BREAK
THE GLASS WALL

And the Lord, he it is that doth go before thee; he will be with thee, he will not fail thee, neither forsake thee: fear not, neither be dismayed.

DEUTERONOMY 31:8

BREAK
THE GLASS WALL

Ennen Reaves Hall

WORD BOOKS, Publisher
Waco, Texas

Library of Congress Catalog Card Number : 75-144369

BREAK THE GLASS WALL, by Ennen Reaves Hall, copyright
© 1971 by Word, Incorporated, Waco, Texas 76703

Printed in the United States of America

Lovingly dedicated to

Sarah P. Brock,
past national president of the
National League of American Pen Women

without whose encouragement this
book might not have been written

Contents

Foreword

THE CHALLENGE to write this book came after reading David's beautiful Psalm 145 where he says, "One generation shall praise thy works to another, and shall declare thy mighty acts." This, we recognize, is the main function of the Bible. It hurdles a generation gap centuries and centuries wide, keeping faith in God alive through preservation of the records of his "mighty acts" for which men like ourselves praised him. As long as faith in him lives, God lives and reigns over our lives.

A thrilling thought. Praise welled up in my heart as I began to relive some of the times God had demonstrated his great love and miraculous power to me when I turned to him in faith—experiences on the whole not unlike those lived by men thousands and thousands of years before they became mine. Experiences where God had seemingly withheld his love also came to mind, but I knew those had been my fault, not his. Although in my sixty-five years of calling myself a Christian I had never doubted God's existence, many times I had let fears exclude me from a sense of his presence as though they had erected a high wall between us. A glass wall, through which each could see the other but which made communication impossible. Yet, in all honesty, there were times when I doubted that he cared enough to even look at me as I groveled in self-pity and fear behind that glass wall.

In time I came to know how wrong I was about that. God always cares, about everything that affects us. It is that knowledge that makes me feel qualified to sing his praises both to those who know him as love and those who do not. In helping and comforting me in my hours of need, he spoke love for all men. It is my joy and privilege to repeat it to all who will listen.

Before gaining understanding through recognition of my own weaknesses, I used to wonder how the wandering children of Israel could accept divine protection and help one day and on the next again become fear-filled. Why could not their faith endure from crisis to crisis?

Life has taught me that this is the way of the human race. We prostrate ourselves in awe and worship while we are in conscious awareness of God's loving presence extending help and comfort. When acute need no longer exists we quickly lose that awareness, and God becomes vague, unreal—little more than a creed or philosophy. We begin to measure God's power by our own human limitations, unable fully to accept his great love as being ours even when we believe it to be; unaware that we have only to give him reality to bring that protective love into manifestation.

The following true incidents from my own experience illustrate this truth. Although I often forgot God, he never forgot me. In recalling these and many other experiences too intimate and too traumatic to include in this book, I am filled with awe. With the psalmist I "sing with the voice of thanksgiving."

If some of the incidents (or miracles, if you prefer the word) seem incredible and wholly undeserved on my part, I can only agree and lift my voice in louder praise.

All Scripture quoted, unless otherwise designated, is from the King James Version.

ENNEN REAVES HALL

1.

The Same
Yesterday and Today

MORE THAN a century after the Crucifixion an un-known author wrote a letter intended to encourage wavering Jewish Christians to remain faithful under trials and persecutions. This letter we know as the Book of Hebrews, and in it is one cryptic message that sums up the importance of using the Holy Scriptures as a guideline for today: "Jesus Christ the same yesterday, and today, and forever" (13:8).

The same Saviour, in a world we think of as changing. Actually we see only outer changes, while the inner man remains the same. The same truths he taught over two thousand years ago light our path today, assuring us of the same divine help given men in ancient times.

Yet without the impact of our personal response those truths are merely words or interesting legends. With that response, they can become instruments for breaking through the glass wall we are prone to erect between ourselves and that Saviour, for rising above the temptations to deny him the power to direct our lives.

How can he be our Saviour without our recognition of him as such? And he is our Saviour for today, for now, if he is the same forever. Although we live in the now, we also live in the forever, a part of the eternality of our Creator-God. In giving us a soul he gave us immortality; in giving us a body with life he gave us a purpose in living, a divine destiny that must be Christ-directed if we are to know the peace of fulfillment.

I am sure that is why the Holy Scriptures have been preserved for us through the dark periods of time when they would have been destroyed had not God had more power than men. They have proved to be as indestructible as God himself in an age when the world is a veritable Tower of Babel, with too much noise and confusion for us to hear the "still small voice" within that once guided men in "paths of righteousness"—in right thinking.

It is our thoughts that determine our destiny, our accomplishments or our failures, our progress or our lack of it. Thoughts dictate decisions, and decisions rule our lives. That is where the Bible has served me and countless other confused pilgrims like me.

It has been more, much more, than a book of rules to live by or a creed with which to be identified. It is more than history or prophecies. It is a mirror in which I see the reflection of my own face when I read of guidance given those with the same problems I have, centuries and centuries before they became mine. The answers I need are always there when faith helps me recognize them.

The Bible, to me, is a voice. The voice of God, speaking words said yesterday to other men in order to save me from mistakes of today. Of now. A voice of love. It is a light in the dark of night, going before me to show me the way God would have me go.

The thought takes me back to a night in an Oklahoma City hospital in 1959, shortly after the publication of my second book. For weeks I had been too busy and too excited in making plans for a happy summer to give any importance to the persistent pain in my left limb. First, there were to be two university seminars on writing in which I was to take part, one in Texas and one in Oklahoma. After that I was to have a vacation in Hawaii, something I had dreamed of for years.

Then suddenly, only one week before I was to give a series of lectures at the Texas university, the pain became too acute to ignore any longer. A visit to an orthopedist indicated an end to all my plans. An old knee injury, apparently suffered in a fall several months before, required immediate surgery. The broken cartilage had worked down into the calf, cutting into ligament and nerve tissue.

As though that weren't enough, the physician detected a flesh tumor high on the thigh of the same limb. Only a biopsy could detect whether or not it was malignant.

His diagnosis left me stunned. Could surgery wait for two weeks? I fairly begged, explaining about the commitments I'd accepted and felt I couldn't avoid keeping at such a late hour. He was sympathetic but firm. Any delay was a grave risk and could result in permanent injury. If a ligament were severed by that displaced cartilage, I might never have use of that limb again.

"Let me think about it tonight," I finally compromised, feeling I had to be alone to quiet my mind and receive divine direction. Surely God had the power to heal me if my faith could accept.

Even more than my ruined vacation and the possibility of a malignant tumor, my responsibility to the two schools weighed heavily on my mind. Both had given me generous publicity, and I would have felt like a traitor to let them down. Not that I could be blamed, yet I did blame myself because I'd ignored warning symptoms for weeks, telling myself I had only to trust in God. At home that night I had to face the truth. Was it faith that had made me ignore that persistent pain, or fear of what I might hear if I consulted a doctor?

So guilt added to my suffering as I tried to find help in prayer. A month, or even less, before, I would have been expendable at those seminars. Replacing me then would have been simple. At this late hour it would be difficult, if not impossible. And it would be very difficult for my replacement to take over without time to plan the workshops I was to direct.

It took a long time that night to quiet my fears, release my guilt and disappointment, and put everything in God's hands. Peace finally came when I recalled words of Jesus: "All things are possible to him that believeth." All things. Then couldn't I avoid that surgery? I believed. God had done so many wonderful things for me. How could I not believe? What he could do once he could do again.

Relieved, almost light-hearted, I slept well that night. The next morning I phoned the surgeon my decision to postpone surgery until my short trips were over. I would take a chance that two weeks wouldn't make any difference. No use telling him I confidently expected to be healed without his help, I had decided (a decision that makes me know now that there was still a little core of fear deep inside me). Yet, perhaps to prove to myself that I was no longer afraid, I went ahead and mailed my check to the travel agency in California through which I had booked my Hawaiian tour. And the checks of two friends who had asked to accompany me.

Both university commitments were successfully concluded, in spite of the fact that the pain in my limb was extremely severe at times, yet bearable. Returning home after the last one, I was busily planning a vacation wardrobe when, without warning, I was wrapped in flames of agony, more unbearable than anything I'd suffered before. A call to my physician resulted in his ordering me straight to the hospital. An hour after checking in, I was wheeled into the operating room.

Upon coming out of the anesthetic, I found my limb in a cast from hip to ankle and myself in such excruciating pain that it was several days later before I even thought of the planned trip. And, guiltily, of the two friends who were happily planning to go with me. Being nonmembers of the writers' organization sponsoring the trip, they could only go as my guests, so their disappointment would be as great as my own.

That I might still carry out those plans never occurred to me. The surgeon had not found a malignant tumor, but the removal of the benign one had required a deep incision, and in addition to the displaced cartilage, he had removed seven calcium spurs from the knee cap. A month or so and I'd be walking again, he had assured me happily.

After he'd left my room, I gave in to bitter disappointment. A month or so—and I'd paid for an expensive trip that was to begin in just six weeks! How could it have happened after I'd felt such assurance that I would not have to have surgery at all? Why had I been allowed to send money for a trip it was evident I couldn't take? This trip had held a special significance for me. It was to have been the fulfillment of a dream I'd shared with my husband through more than twenty years of marriage. His dream, really. Having lived in the Islands before I'd known him, he loved to talk of places he'd show me—some day. That day had not come for him, for he'd died twenty-five years before, but I had the warm feeling that he'd still go with me in spirit, that together we would visit the places of tropical beauty he had hoped to show me.

Childish tears ran down my cheeks as I relinquished the dream. "I can't go, Mike," I whispered. "I guess it just wasn't meant to be."

A telephone call to the travel agency brought the information that cancellation was possible if received in writing within ten days. Having accepted disappointment, my mind also accepted continued pain, and that night I lay sleepless in spite of sedation, so depressed my suffering seemed intensified. Unable to turn because of the cast, haunted by the thought of my friends' disappointment and the feeling that somehow I had proven faithless, I gave in to self-pity. Like Job, I kept crying out silently, Why, God? Why did this happen to me now? And how can I honor you if I have to walk leaning on a cane after this?

That was my deepest fear—that I might never be able to trust that damaged knee again. Although I was almost sixty-nine, God had given me far better health since I'd put my whole life in his hands than I'd ever had as a young woman, making it possible for me to enjoy the same activities as friends many years younger than myself. I didn't want that changed.

Toward morning I fell into a restless sleep, and it was then the dream came. Yet it was so real I can hardly think of it as a dream. It was more like an experience, for all five senses were involved. In the dream I stood in impenetrable blackness, alone and terrified. Although I couldn't distinguish anything, the sounds and smells identified the locale as a swamp like the ones I had seen in Louisiana. Cold, slimy water lapping about my ankles, the musky odor peculiar to such places, the unmistakable noise made by crocodiles thrashing about close by—all warned me of my perilous position.

Although my knowledge of swamps was limited, I knew that the depth of water varied greatly at different points. It was only ankle-deep where I stood, but the evidence of savage crocodiles so near warned me not to change my position by as much as a step. Not only could the water be dangerously deep just a few feet away, but poisonous reptiles as well as crocodiles infested such places.

While I stood quaking with fear and wondering what to do, I became aware of a light, seemingly far out in the swamp. Just a tiny glow in the night but a moving one, as though it were being carried by someone I could not see. It must be a lantern, I decided, such as my father used to carry when abroad at night. And it was seemingly moving in a straight line, as though the one who carried it knew exactly where he was going.

Excited hope filled me. That person must know the way out of this terrible place. Surely if I followed him, staying in line with the light, I'd get out also.

Carefully, slowly, I placed one foot exactly before the other, my eyes fixed on the light that kept moving and yet didn't seem to be gaining on me. To my vast relief, I discovered as I kept moving cautiously that I was on a solid ledge of some kind, perhaps a concrete wall or dam barely covered by water. The sounds and smells of the swamp, and the feel of the slimy water, were still around me but my fear was gone. Some one ahead of me knew the way and I had only to follow.

A voice, somewhere deep within me, awoke me just as day was breaking. It was as clear and distinct as the other sensations had been, and it was saying, "Thy word shall be a lamp unto my feet" (Ps. 119:105).

His Word, I thought wonderingly, wide awake. Yes, that could have been the light I saw. But what was it revealing to me? With all my heart I wanted to know.

Then suddenly I did know, as clearly as I'd known how to get out of that swamp in my dream, for another verse of Scripture came into my mind, words Paul wrote to a young man named Timothy: "God hath not given us the spirit of fear; but of power, and of love, and of a sound mind" (2 Tim. 1:7).

The spirit of power—then why had I been accepting continued helplessness? *The spirit of love*—why had I entertained the thought of failing my friends? *The spirit of a sound mind*—that was what I'd thought I was listening to, but how wrong I'd been. All the teaching of the Bible, all past experiences, reminded me that only faith gives soundness to our human minds, not logic and reason based on negativity. That dream must have been a form of divine communication, telling me Divine Mind saw no reason why I couldn't claim the happy experience he had offered me. Hadn't he known this would happen to me when he permitted me to make those plans?

By the time my physician made his morning visit, every doubt was resolved. Quietly confident, I asked him how soon I could get out of that cast and begin therapeutic treatments. "I'm going to Hawaii, after all," I announced, as though everything were settled. "But I'm not going leaning on a cane or crutches."

"Good for you," he surprised me by saying. "If you want to go that badly you'll probably make it, although I do advise the cane for awhile."

After the cast was removed and the painful process of learning to walk again was begun, the trip didn't seem so important, for pain and weakness were still mine. But it was very, very important that I follow the light I'd been shown. Even when I was tempted, I couldn't give up. It was as though I'd made a bargain with God and had to keep it.

Less than a month after leaving the hospital I flew to Los Angeles to meet my party. And I went without either crutches or a cane. God's victory, not mine.

On my return six weeks later, my elated surgeon told me, "I wasn't at all sure you could do it, but that trip was the very best therapy I could have ordered. The walking and climbing on and off buses prevented stiffening of that knee, something that often happens to elderly people after such surgery."

The spirit of a sound mind that trusts in God's guidance! The wonderful, marvelous ways of God, always ready to guide us into our good! Not only did he guide me into accepting a happy and profitable experience he had designed for me, but he made me the instrument of his love in giving the same happy experience to the friends I loved.

It is still with awe that I recall that neither of those friends lived very long after that trip. One was stricken with a malignancy and during her long invalidism found much joy in reliving those happy weeks, looking at pictures and mementos. The other developed a heart condition that forced her to curtail activities, and she never tired of talking about the joyous experience we had shared. So how can I ever stop thanking God for showing me the light of truth that night?

He does work in just such ways, my Bible tells me. He often

spoke to men in dreams in Bible times. Who can say he no longer does?

One thing I know and can never doubt—God does go before us, in any situation we are called upon to experience, to light the way. His Word of love is always ours to guide us through darkness and into the light of day. *"Our Praise"*

and may we at all times claim this assurance Deuteronomy 31:8

2.
Finding Self-Identity

L AST SPRING when I started to replant a flower bed I was surprised to find it already carpeted with tiny green shoots. What were they? Nothing I had planted, for I had only recently remulched the soil. Leaving them undisturbed, I was able before long to identify them as oriental poppies I had planted over two years before. When they had failed to sprout within a few months, I had given them up and planted some annuals in the bed. This was repeated several times, the poppies being completely forgotten. Now at last they were pushing through the ground, hardy and strong. A month later the bed was a riot of color.

Looking at those colorful pompons, I was filled with awe at the thought of all that beauty lying dormant in the ground for so long before life stirred in the tiny seed, causing them to start pushing toward light.

Surely nothing speaks more eloquently of a living God than does a seed. Just a tiny, dry, and seemingly dead husk, yet there is trapped within it vibrant life, the germ of growth and fruitage, of glowing color and beauty such as man cannot imitate with all the artistry of which he is capable.

In that little seed there is also an instinctive faith in its destiny, making the process of growth an automatic thing, a continuous reaching toward self-expression. This instinctive faith was what had finally brought my poppy seeds out of the darkness of the ground and into beauty.

Yet, as awe-inspiring as it is to see fruition come from a seemingly dead husk called a seed, it is even more inspiring to see an unresponsive, wasted life suddenly begin to bear fruit. History is filled with such stories. Scores of men and women, viewed by the world as failures or social misfits until they turned to God as the directing power in their lives, have recorded outstanding accomplishments or undergone a complete change in personality.

One case in point is Paul, the inspiring biblical evangelical writer. Endowed with great intellect and education, the young Jew known as Saul of Tarsus had chosen to express violence and hatred in the very name of God. Saul, on his way to Damascus one day to pursue his bitter persecution of the followers of the crucified Jesus, was struck by blinding light. At that moment he was changed from a biased and wrathful instrument of vengeance to a zealous exponent of justice and love, a teacher of truths. As Paul, the new man he became, he wrote to the same organized groups he'd once persecuted so vigorously inspiring letters that have become immortal, rated second only to the recorded teachings of Jesus.

Outwardly, Saul had become a new man—Paul. Yet what his world saw as change was actually only development. Growth. Like my tiny seeds, his true self had only lain dormant within the dry husk of a man the world of his day had been seeing. The potential for what he finally became had been there all the time. It is there in all men, because God, limitless power and limitless love, created us in his image, or likeness. It is a cosmic law that like begets like; so it is our inherent destiny to express our Creator—to grow and develop into reflections of him.

To achieve our true potential we must first know ourselves. This eternal truth the philosopher Socrates was teaching four hundred years before Jesus walked among men, teaching the same thing. But Jesus went further than any teacher before him had ever done. He demonstrated the power he said lies within us when we know ourselves as children of God, when we let ourselves become his expression of love.

The hunger for this true self-expression is paramount in every human heart until it is lost through negation. When Jesus said, "I am the light of the world," he was not referring to his personality, but to the truths which he taught, the love which he felt for all men.

He was identifying with God. Just as seed will not grow if denied light, neither can the inner man develop without this God-awareness.

Conditions neither diffuse nor prevent God's light that fosters growth. A modern evangelist of tremendous influence saw and began to reach for that light while in prison, lying on the concrete floor of a solitary cell, half dead from the beating he'd received at the hands of a guard.

Every one who has heard Starr Daily recount his remarkable experience, so comparable to that of Paul, knows that his light dawned when his thoughts turned to his praying father and to the God worshipped by his parent. It was the memory of early teachings, long ignored but not forgotten, that crystalized the resolution of this untutored and friendless social outcast to start expressing his highest potentials instead of keeping them hidden in darkness.

The desire to grow and express our highest and best is a cry that never fails to reach God, and it is often in times of human extremity that we first give voice to it. Then we echo the words of Jonah, who lived three days and nights in a whale's belly: "When my soul fainted within me I remembered the Lord: and my prayer came in unto thee, into thine holy temple" (Jonah 2:7).

That so many souls are fainting all around us is an indictment against us who call ourselves Christians. We proclaim our belief in divine power, but we offer so little evidence of the influence of that kind of power in our personal lives: Jesus taught that our lives would show its effects when we believe in it. Even as we speak praises to God we decry the possibility of miracles such as fill the pages of the book we call God's Word. Are we offering our youth a God that changes with the times, a God as limited in his ability to perform as is our weak humanity? If so, are we not stifling in them the desire for the Light by which to grow, offering them little incentive to "remember the Lord" when their souls faint within them?

We have given our younger generation much in the way of material things but little to make life meaningful and challenging. So the eternal search for happiness, for self-identification, has been intensified, often in ways that can only lead to tragic failure. Jesus pointed out the way that search should lead when he told questioning, skeptical Pharisees that he had the light. And he added, confidently,

"I know whence I come and whither I go" (John 8:14).

Although human like us (Heb. 2:16–18), Jesus, through recalling the teachings of Moses, found a strength beyond his humanity when he searched for and received his answers during his forty days' sojourn in the wilderness. God has continued to preserve these same teachings for every generation since; yet there are those today who would make these same teachings a forbidden study, and there are countless others who give such a study no place in their lives.

Not that we can, or should, attempt to analyze or to rationalize God. He just is, as Paul wrote to a young man named Timothy, "King of kings and Lord of lords; . . . dwelling in the light which no man can approach unto; whom no man hath seen, nor can see; to whom be honor and power everlasting" (1 Tim. 6:15–16).

The teaching we can and should give our restless youth is not what God is, but how he is—a God of power, as concerned about the now as the hereafter; a God of love, ready to help us attain joy and peace and fulfillment in the now when there is total faith in him. We must give them a constructive faith, such as is described in the first verse of the eleventh chapter of Hebrews, "Faith is the substance of things hoped for, the evidence of things not seen"—a faith that does not demand evidence of God's reality, but is eager to become that evidence.

Only such a faith in God can instill faith in ourselves that contributes to security and ends the restless search for self-identification, for the need to prove to ourselves that we can meet the competition of a seemingly ruthless world, for the need for approval of others. A faith that makes it possible to achieve fulfillment when measured only by the standards set by God. A faith that releases the limitless power of God.

My neighbor's son is only ten but has already become a source of disturbance in our quiet neighborhood. When he wandered over to my patio one evening, I found it a little difficult to welcome him at first as I recalled the stray cat he'd drowned in my fish pool, the garbage he'd thrown into the swimming pool, and the way he amused himself by throwing rocks at passing cars.

When he opened conversation by asking what I was doing, sitting there by myself, I looked back at the particularly colorful sunset I'd been enjoying and forgot my annoyance at his intrusion.

"I've been watching God paint a gorgeous picture in the sky," I answered. "Look! Did you ever see anything more beautiful?"

If I had unconsciously wanted to start an argument I had succeeded. "That's just an old sunset," he said, his tone reflecting youth's scorn of my illiterate generation. "Besides, what makes you think God is real? He's just something grownups have made up to scare you with."

Agnosticism in one so young left me speechless for a moment. Then I helplessly replied with a counterquestion. "What makes you think he isn't real, Bobby?"

"That's easy." He sounded almost triumphant. "Nobody's ever seen him or heard him or anything. So how could he be real?"

Here was a challenge I couldn't ignore. Yet what could I say to such a young skeptic? There was such a wide generation gap between us—more than sixty years wide. How could I hope to establish communication? Then he challenged me again, and everything was forgotten except compassion, for there was hunger in Bobby's voice and in his eyes.

"Did you ever see this God you say paints pictures in the sky? Or hear him answer people when they talk to him?"

Suddenly I was eight again and all the doubts this child was voicing were mine, except I did not dare mention such doubts to my minister father or my devout mother. My doubts, however, had nothing to do with the existence of God. No one in my father's family could question the reality of the God he preached so zealously. But so much emphasis was put upon the punishment he dealt sinners and there was so much secret guilt in my heart because of my distrust of what I thought of as Papa's God that I felt completely alienated from him. He didn't like me any more than I did him, I decided when I was six and my prayers for my sick baby sister to whom I was devoted went unheeded. When she died, the friends and church members who came to offer sympathy all spoke of God's will, increasing my feeling of complete rejection.

I didn't like Papa's God, I decided. Why did he answer the prayers of some but not all? Was it because he couldn't do the things my father said he could, or because he wouldn't?

"Well?" My young guest's voice jerked me back from the past. "Did this God you say is real ever say anything to you?"

"Yes," I said, feeling a deep well of joy inside me as I replied. "He's spoken to me many times. A time I remember especially was when I was about your age. I'd disobeyed my mother by taking her good scissors outdoors to cut paper dolls and forgetting to take them back to the dresser drawer in which she kept them."

Pausing to take a deep breath, I felt as though I'd gone back through time and was again playing in what I liked to think of as my secret hideout, a small cleared space among tall hollyhocks in the backyard of an Indian Territory parsonage. It even seemed as if I could hear my mother's sharp voice bouncing across the yard toward me. "Ennen? Have you been using my new scissors? They're not in the dresser drawer. I'll give you five minutes to find them, young lady."

When my mother's voice took on that sharp a tone we knew trouble threatened. Conscience-stricken, I'd hurriedly searched the area where I might have left them, then ran into the house to see for myself that my mother was right. The scissors were not in their accustomed place.

"Well?" Bobby's impatient boyish voice broke into my thoughts. "What did God say to you about that? That he was going to strike you dead for being bad?"

"Oh, no," I replied smilingly, knowing I spoke the truth, phenomenal as it sounded. "He told me how to find the scissors."

My audience was all attention now. "No kidding?"

"No kidding, Bobby. After my mother and I both failed to find them, I'd run back to my playhouse among some hollyhocks, trying to delay punishment as long as possible. There I asked God to help me because I knew it would be hard for my mother to get more good scissors in our small town. Then I heard words as plain as I hear you now. At first I thought the hollyhocks whispered them, but I knew flowers couldn't talk. So it had to be God that said, "Go back and look in the dresser drawer again.""

"But they couldn't have been there if you and your mother had already looked," he interrupted me.

"Yet they were," I assured him, "and right in plain view."

Again I moved back through time and felt the surge of joy that had welled up in me that long ago day at sight of those bright shears. I knew in my heart I'd found more than a lost household article. I'd found a God who cared about me, after all, as undeserving as I felt myself to be. That the scissors had been miraculously placed there for me I had no doubts whatever, nor have I been able to doubt in the sixty and more years since, for I have never found any other explanation.

Bobby was impressed, also. "Gee whillikers," he exclaimed. "Sounds like magic."

"It was magic," I answered. "And that's really what God is, Bobby. Beautiful magic when we really believe in him."

He stood up, looking a little stunned with awe. "Gosh, what did you say to make the magic work?"

I smiled, thinking of the childish challenge I'd flung at the Almighty that day, but thought it wiser not to tell Bobby the exact words I'd used. Instead I simplified the very unorthodox prayer I'd made. "I just told him I knew he could help me."

He started to leave, then turned back to say, a little sheepishly, "I guess I'm sorry about that old cat. You think I can learn to work magic like that?"

"You can if you really believe in it," I assured him. "Try it sometime, Bobby."

Watching him walk away, still with that look of awe in his eyes, I knew I had planted a little seed. I whispered a prayer that it might germinate and bear fruit some day. Surely belief in the magic power of God's love is what today's youth is searching for, starving for; yet seldom are they offered anything but a dry theology or a creed that contributes only to a sense of well-being while falling far short of our needs. All of us yearn to identify with a power greater than our weak humanity, to find the peace Jesus said he came to leave with us, to see the miracles he said believers on him would be able to do.

Sitting on a spectator's bench labeled "retirement," watching the growth of religious institutions that seem to have little influence upon a chaotic world, I am concerned that the Christianity of Jesus may be regressing instead of advancing. Is it not possible that in giving so much emphasis to human relations and accomplishments we are denying ourselves the close personal relationship with God that the Saviour advocated? Denying our generation of youth, and generations yet to come, the security found in the "magic" my small neighbor hungers for? Denying young and old the most exciting, most challenging adventures life offers—explorations into faith—because we are showing them few or no miracles such as Moses demonstrated to his people and Jesus to his followers?

"Choose ye this day whom you will serve," Joshua told a fearful people standing within sight of the land of their dreams. In using the word "serve" he was urging them to serve God not through acts of self-denial nor the amassing of a record of good deeds but through serving themselves, obtaining a better way of life than the nomadic existence they had known. They were to find self-fulfillment through faith.

If we today rob ourselves of such a life it is by choice. The only service God asks of us is that we let him serve us.

3.

Perfect Love in Expression

A BIBLE STORY of Zacchaeus, the diminutive tax collector who climbed a tree to see Jesus, has always intrigued me. Perhaps it was what influenced me to climb into an apple tree to wait for the end of the world when I was twelve, having been convinced by a zealous Sunday school teacher that it was imminent.

My tree experience differed from that of the despised publican, however. He came down from his leafy perch a changed man after seeing Jesus and realized his own deep need for what the most noted man in all Galilee was offering him—love and friendship and a sense of belonging. When I came down out of my tree, I was still a confused and frightened girl because I had been shown only my need of escape from the eternal torture so vividly portrayed by my spiritual mentor.

Recalling this early incident, I find myself thinking how different life might have been if, instead of the voice of fear, I had heard the voice of love that day, as had Zacchaeus. Beyond doubt, the same Christ Jesus stood under my tree, eager to call to me in love, but I could not hear him above the tumult in my heart. I identified God only with justice and retribution; I saw myself as a sinner because I did not want to bargain with him over my soul's salvation.

So there was revolt in my heart then for the same reason there is a religious revolt among youth today—because I had been given a philosophy of fear, with little evidence of the fact that the most challenging and most exciting experience life offers is exactly what was given a sinful publican when he scrambled down out of his tree to meet Jesus. Had this truth been emphasized for me, I would have left my spectator's seat as joyously as Zacchaeus left his when Jesus offered him a whole new way of life: not a life of self-denial, such as I pictured, but of self-fulfillment; not of separation from a world I found exciting, but of involvement in making it the kind of world I wanted.

What our world is like is determined only by ourselves, I was to learn, each of us creating whatever conditions we identify with. Even though God is ever ready to demonstrate the greatness and unlimited riches of his love, he can do so only with our consent. In creating man in the image of himself, he gave us creative powers of thought.

What else is faith but thought? Thus we have the power to give reality to either our spiritual nature, attuned to divine love, or to our humanity only and to whatever limiting conditions surround us.

In teaching that "God is love," Jesus was saying much more than that God loves men. God, he made plain, is the very essence of love, the law of love in operation, as unfailing and infallible as all the laws of physics that govern the universe. Available to all of us, indiscriminately, yet as warmly personal as a mother's tender care when we attune to this Love by giving love to that God which was one with a man like ourselves called Jesus.

This dual identity of Jesus was a stumbling block in my path for many years. In my youth God was presented as being so remote and withdrawn from man that he found it impossible to forgive our rejection of him as the ruler of our lives until his Son suffered all the agony men could inflict to win that forgiveness for us. How could anyone love such a hard-hearted God?

Having abandoned my early childish concept of God as something like Aladdin's magic lamp, my teen years found me almost violently resisting the "salvation" my father and his well-meaning church members kept urging upon me. No real reason was given me for loving either God or his Son except as a means of escape from eternal punishment. Because youth is inclined to be more basically honest than adulthood, and, not having perfected the art of diplomacy and deception, I felt strongly that I was demeaning myself by publicly confessing to being a sinner and cheapening God by attempting to bargain with him in order to avoid an unhappy fate in the dim and (I hoped) distant future.

From the time I was twelve, I had taken an active part in church life, often feeling a little martyred for sitting at the wheezy reed organ, pumping furiously on the foot pedals to keep air flowing through its leaky pipes, when I might have been sitting on a rear seat with a date like other girls my age. What more did God want of me that I should be classified as a sinful person?

In spite of my doubts and confusion, even secret resentment, I yielded to pressure and joined the church during a spring revival shortly after I reached sixteen. My parents were overjoyed that I had finally surrendered my life to God, but I harbored a deep sense of guilt, knowing it was not God but my father's wishes that I had surrendered to.

Instead of joy in my heart over my decision, there was only a sick dread of what that decision obligated me to do—be immersed in the river a mile from town. How I dreaded the very thought! For one thing, my fear of water was almost a phobia; for another, I had watched river baptizings all my life and always suffered acute embarrassment for the women and girls when they waded out of the water with their hair plastered to their heads, their wet clothing clinging revealingly to their bodies.

When a heavy spring rain sent the river almost out of its banks, I was relieved to have even a temporary reprieve. One Saturday morning I won my mother's consent to go horseback riding with three other girls, after giving her my promise that I would not let anyone see me riding astride, even though I had to use my brother's saddle and his spirited horse that was blind in one eye.

To make sure my modesty would be preserved, my usually frugal mother suggested I wear my best skirt because it had a wide flounce, and a new green petticoat she had just made me, also with a ruffle.

To be able to keep my promise the easiest way, we headed for a country lane little used by farmers going in to market. There I changed my position from an awkward side-sitting, definitely hard to maintain in a man's saddle, to the man-style the other girls were using. Hardly had I settled into the more comfortable position when the girl riding ahead of me called back a warning: "Look out, here comes a man!"

The rider was jogging towards us at a fair rate of speed so I started to make a quick changeover to my first position. While I was in the very act of swinging my limb over the saddle horn, the wind, seldom entirely still in Oklahoma, blew a scrap of paper against my horse's foreleg. He shied violently toward the barbed-wire fence beside which I'd been riding. Unfortunately the fence was on the animal's blind side. The next thing I knew I was being dragged at the heels of my running horse, one foot still caught in the stirrup.

The man, innocent cause of the accident, stopped my horse and with the help of my companions got me back into the saddle. It no longer mattered that I had to sit astride in order to stay on. With one of the girls riding ahead to alert my mother, one leading my horse, and the third riding beside me to keep me from falling off, we managed to make it back home.

In a state of complete shock, I was only vaguely aware of being hurt, puzzled by the blood streaming down one arm and the fact that my wide skirts no longer covered my knees. Most disturbing of all was something wet and slimy lying across my cheek, which my numb hand was unable to brush off. Pain had not yet begun its vicious onslaught when we reached home and Mamma took charge.

Usually calm and efficient in a crisis, my poor mother's self-control almost deserted her at sight of what was left of me. Hearing her talk over the telephone, I wondered at the way her voice shook and at what she was saying. "Doctor, she's cut to ribbons on a barbed-wire fence. One ear is lying on her cheek, just held by a bit of skin. Isn't there any way you can get out here?"

Until then I'd forgotten that the creek that divided the town was at flood stage and that one end of the wooden bridge had been carried away the day before. But by then I was drifting off into space on waves of pain and hardly knew when my mother and my friends went to work on me.

It was hours later before the doctor arrived, having resorted to the use of a boat improvised by my brother. By that time I was stupefied by the paregoric Mamma had been pouring into me, and, according to my brother, I looked like a well-preserved mummy in strips of what had been one of my mother's best sheets.

After unwinding me and suturing deep cuts on one arm and leg, the doctor shocked me into reality by saying there was nothing he could do about the severed ear. "It's cut off so close to her head there's nothing to sew to but bone," he was telling Mamma. "Only thing to do is clip it clear off."

"You will not!" Plainly Mamma was ready to go to battle. "That girl's not going through life with one ear. At least we can leave it alone and give it a chance to grow back on."

"That's too risky," the doctor protested. "It will have to stay bandaged without being disturbed for weeks, and blood poisoning is sure to set in. Besides, there's nothing there for it to grow to. Better for her to lose an ear than her life."

I'm not sure how long the argument lasted, but after the physician gave up and left, my mother tried to reassure me. "Don't you worry, child. The good Lord healed the ear of that soldier when Peter cut it off, didn't he? I don't see why he can't heal yours if we keep faith in him."

Through a sleepless night I kept hearing her words, but without much comfort. Mamma didn't know I was still a sinner in spite of having joined the church, that I didn't really care about my soul and didn't want to be baptized. Why should God do anything for me?

It must have been nearly morning when a comforting thought did occur to me. I was going over the few details given about that incident in the garden of Gethsemane when a fact I'd been overlooking suddenly made sharp impact. That soldier whose ear Peter had cut off in his defense of Jesus was no better than I! He was the enemy of Jesus, trying to arrest him! Yet the Lord had tenderly replaced his ear and healing had taken place. If it could happen to a man like that, couldn't it happen to me? Such a warm glow filled my pain-wracked body at the thought that I drifted off to sleep murmuring, "Thank you, Lord . . . thank you."

Three weeks or so later, after my mother had soaked the blood-encrusted head bandages until they became pliant, the doctor gingerly unwound them, shaking his head dolefully. "I'm almost afraid to look," he kept mumbling. "This ought to have been treated right along like the other places."

When the damaged ear was finally exposed, he stared at it incredulously. "This beats anything I ever saw," he said, over and over. "All healed over without even a scar. I'll say you sure are a lucky young lady."

There were plenty of scars on my arm and limb, some of which I still carry, more than sixty years later. But I knew it wasn't luck that had restored my ear. It was God's love. The thought was the most thrilling I'd ever known.

A few days later my brother drove me out to what he called the scene of the slaughter, hoping we could prove or disprove our mother's theory that I'd fallen over the fence and been pulled through those spiked wires. It seemed incredible when we saw that fence. Made to keep hogs from wandering out of their feeding ground, it had several strands, not planned for height but put close enough together to discourage even half-grown pigs from trying to wriggle through. Impossible that a human my size could have been pulled through without even more damage than I'd suffered.

Yet there was the evidence—bits of green cloth, sun- and rain-faded now, clinging to barbs on the inside of the fence, plus the tattered remains of what had been a high-topped button shoe, about which we had wondered. It, too, lay inside the pasture.

A miracle, I kept thinking as we drove home. And I'd stopped believing in them!

It was like another miracle to discover my dread of being baptized was gone, also. Fear returned, however, the Sunday afternoon I stood on the river bank while my mother pinned my several skirts together so they wouldn't float when I entered the water. Other female candidates were being similarly prepared while my father baptized several male converts.

That river looked awfully high and swift to me. I found myself shivering violently in spite of the hot summer day. When it came our turn to wade out to midstream where my father waited for us, I wanted nothing so much as to break the human chain we made by joining hands and run and run. Then I was being fairly pulled along by braver souls into water almost to my waist. When my feet struck something, a hole or rock, and I stumbled and almost went under, I had to fight against sheer panic. As I regained my balance with the help of my companions, I wondered wildly if they could hear the voice babbling inside my head: *Please, God, I can't! I can't! Please get me out of this!*

Then it was my turn to move close to Papa. His hands were strong, his voice gentle, as he told me just when to hold my breath and how to bend my knees when he lowered me into the water. He must have sensed my panic for he ended his brief instructions by saying, "Just hold to my hand and trust God."

Trust God? Until then I hadn't really associated God with the rite. It was merely a church-required ordinance, something I must submit to in order to be identified with the saved. At Papa's words, like a flash of light, I had a mental picture of Jesus standing in the Jordan river, and I saw the rite also was identified with the one who had given me back my ear.

The realization brought a rush of joy, as though a fountain had bubbled up inside me. When Papa said, "Hold your breath," and lowered my relaxed body into the water, it seemed to me that tender hands caressed my face instead of slightly muddy water.

It was over in seconds but the joy remained, so real and deep that I would not have been surprised if a dove had flown out of the brassy sky to light on my shoulder.

Many times in the years that followed I tried without success to recapture the shining translucency of that moment's experience in the river. From this vantage point of hindsight I know I touched God that day in that brief flight into space. For that short period of realization, he had been as real as the parent who stood beside me and held my hands. Until then God's reality for me had been vaguely identified with my performance, but that afternoon he assumed a personality I could never again wholly lose sight of. Such is the holding power of divine love.

Paul's statement to the church at Rome, "All have sinned and come short of the glory of God," had been my stumbling block, making me feel beyond the power of divine protection. Today, while still knowing myself among the sinful of the world, I no longer interpret the statement as referring to carnal sins of commission or omission, as it was preached to me.

Paul, I feel, was reminding those early Christians—and us today —that it is a sin against God, a betrayal of our Savior, to "come short" of the glorious experience a God-directed life can be; that rapport found in awareness of such divine direction is a power in itself, removing human limitations by lifting the surrendered heart above conditions and circumstances.

Praise God!

Insight that brings joy - peace and sweet assurance

4.

The Illusion of Freedom

THE ATTEMPTS of the younger generation to declare their freedom from traditional customs of the world in which they live, from parental authority, and, in some instances, from even legal restraints are both tragic and amusing to an older and experienced generation. A popular concept is that older people cannot understand the rebellious drives of youth, but it is a wholly wrong concept, generally speaking. We understand all too well.

The road many are choosing in their search for self-identity and individuality is not a new one, as some like to think. Rather, it is a path hardened by countless numbers of feet that have used it in the same fruitless search, only to find that the road has no end. It goes nowhere.

Freedom is not a condition. It is a state of mind, and it is attained only when we recognize that none of us was created to live on an island of self. Each is a part of a divine whole, and thus all are dependent upon each other. To see ourselves as separate is to accept separation from our Creator-God and thus deny our true selves even as we attempt to express such a self.

Jesus once told men longing for political freedom, "Ye shall know the truth, and the truth shall make you free" (John 8:32). When his listeners protested loudly he added, "If the Son therefore shall make you free, ye shall be free indeed" (8:36).

Truth, the Son, made synonymous. What truth then frees us? Identification with God, with love for all men such as Jesus demonstrated.

Jesus made another oblique statement about freedom when he told his disciples, "He that findeth his life shall lose it: and he that loseth his life for my sake shall find it" (Matt. 10: 39). Growing up in the church, I was taught that he was warning his dedicated followers not to expect rewards while in the world but that they would be rewarded after death if they remained faithful. Though I was reared in this doctrine, I can no longer accept it literally.

To find and lose one's life, I feel he was saying, is to attempt to live apart from God, to assert our independence of his spiritual laws in a world too complex for any of us to walk alone. Jesus was love personified. To follow him, he was telling those early disciples, they must also become love.

In telling them, he was also telling us. Nothing he said was spoken for one group only, or for one period of time. His love and his affinity with God transcended personalities and time. Thus he spoke to all men in all walks of life and in all ages to come. And he was telling us all that if we let the Christ of God be the ruling power in our lives, we shall find the true meaning of life, of true happiness and security. Then we are free of all crippling influences, no matter what circumstances under which we live.

Much is being said today about sexual freedom. This type of freedom is the most illusory of all. Without love such freedom becomes license, and both sacred and secular history prove the fallacy of attempting to find freedom in self-indulgence. A breakdown of moral standards caused the fall of Rome, according to many historians, and the Bible is filled with stories of disasters brought about by the compromise with ideals, just as are our news media of today.

In the divine creation, sex was made an expression of love. Without love it becomes an expression of our baser nature; yet with love both the man and woman relinquish their personal freedom, for they are no longer individuals, but each a part of the other. In this God–ordained relationship, we see a perfect illustration of finding one's life through losing it. Love makes us free, even as it enslaves us, for there is no love or self-fulfillment unless there is willingness on the part of both husband and wife to sacrifice personal freedom.

Had I been taught this truth I would not have entered into marriage at the age of nineteen with the delusion that I was finding a whole new world of freedom such as I craved. Like the prodigal son in the parable Jesus told, and like countless numbers of prodigal youths today, I thought I wanted to be free to live my own life without parental intervention, to experience pleasures that had always been forbidden me, to find self-expression—things I felt I was being denied.

Because of the teaching I'd been given that all men were conceived in sin, I naturally separated sexual experience from God and felt that in choosing to marry Mike I was renouncing Him. So there was guilt in my heart as I took my marriage vows, and nothing can separate us from God more effectively than a guilt complex.

My devoted and well-meaning parents added to this sense of guilt with their warnings that I, a Christian girl, could not expect to find happiness with a man of the world ten years my senior, who frankly admitted he subscribed to no religious belief. Also he smoked "coffin nails," as cigarettes were called in that day; he was virtually a stranger, for I'd only known him three months; he'd led a nomadic life after serving two years in the Philippines during the Spanish–American war; while I had never been more than sixty miles away from the small town in which I'd been reared.

Because fears are communicative, my parents' fears became mine. They added to the guilt I took to the altar—a guilt that increased each time I found happiness in my husband's arms. When I became pregnant the fears and guilt multiplied, robbing me of the joy that should have been mine in anticipating motherhood, the happiest experience God can bestow upon a woman.

Perhaps these confused emotions were responsible in part for the fact that the whole nine months of pregnancy were accompanied with almost violent nausea, so that Mike yielded to my mother's pleas and we moved back into my parents' home by the end of the fourth month. There I stayed in hiding, as did all pregnant women in those days, feeling shame and embarrassment at what I had brought upon myself, comforted only by Mike's joy and pride. Yet Mike, as my worried mother often reminded me, did not have to endure the ordeal I faced. Although she had given birth to nine children she entertained grave fears for her young daughter and did not realize how adversely those fears were affecting me.

Perhaps I was unconsciously accepting defeat before labor began early one October Friday morning. By midday Saturday I was still in the throes of violent agony, convinced that God was punishing me by throwing me into a fiery furnace like the ones ordered for Shadrach, Meshach, and Abednego by a king of Babylon. Only God was not going to deliver me as he had the three faithful Hebrews. Why should he, when I had not been faithful as were they?

The Bible story kept recurring to me during seventy-two hours of excruciating labor, because of an incident the day before my ordeal began. Papa, who had been starting a fire in the kitchen range, thoughtlessly added kerosene to smoldering wood, and his shirt sleeve caught on fire. Mike had walked in just in time to tear the flaming cloth off Papa's arm, moving so quickly that both of them only suffered minor burns.

As Mamma and I brought bandages and liniment, Papa reassured us. "It doesn't amount to anything. But thank God Mike came in just when he did."

Mike said teasingly, for he and Papa had become fast friends, "Looks like a good man like you wouldn't need anyone. Nothing happened to the three guys in the fiery furnace, did it?"

My father was too English to respond quickly to a joke. "That's right," he replied unsmiling, "nothing did. But it wasn't their fault they were thrown into the fire, and it was mine that I threw that kerosene in."

His words still lingered in my mind as Sunday came. The occasional whiffs of chloroform I was allowed by the old physician did little to alleviate my agony, and the conviction grew that my baby was not destined to be born. As Papa had said about his own narrow escape, it was all my fault, a punishment I had brought upon myself. From time to time I tried to say something like that to Mike, who had not left my bedside in the two days and nights, but when I opened my tightly clenched mouth only the screams I'd been fighting to hold back came out.

Sometime during that endless Sunday a soft cloud seemed to be smothering the flames in which I'd been trapped, and I sank into its velvety cushion, the thought of rest exquisitely sweet. Far over my head voices were floating around but words didn't register until

I heard my doctor say, "It's no use, Mike. I've waited as long as I dare. I may be able to save her, but not the baby. Its head is lodged, and she's built too narrow to let it pass."

My husband's fear-stricken voice broke in, "Then save her, Doc. And hurry."

Vaguely I realized what those words cost Mike. He had been almost deliriously happy about this child. Reared an orphan himself, he coveted the family ties he'd never known. Now there wouldn't be any baby for us, but at least I could rest . . .

The clink of instruments being dropped into a pan of boiling water jerked me off the cloud and back into the furnace. Simultaneously I became aware of another sound—the slow pacing of heavy feet up and down the hallway outside my room. That had to be Papa. Instinctively I knew he was praying for me as he paced up and down. The thought jerked me into full awareness of what was about to take place, and hope was a strong stimulant. Maybe God would hear Papa's prayers and save the son Mike wanted so much!

As though in answer to the thought, I heard other words spoken, as clearly as if the speaker had crossed centuries of time and stood beside me: "Our God, whom we serve, is able to deliver us" (Dan. 3:17). Words spoken in defiance of a heathen king, now spoken compassionately to a suffering girl centuries later made it seem that God himself was speaking his forgiveness and love—as indeed he was. Here was the reassurance I'd longed for. I began screaming a protest at what the physician proposed to do. At least I thought I screamed, although later Mike told me the words came only in a frantic whisper: "No, no, Mike! Don't let him kill our baby! Let me keep trying. Papa is praying, and God will help me."

"Can't we wait a little longer, Doc?" Mike fairly begged.

"It's your decision," I heard the doctor reply. "But it's no use. Her strength has given out."

My strength, yes. But I had finally turned to a strength beyond my humanity, accepting the power of God as mine in this battle for the life he had entrusted to me.

The rest of that day and half the night is something I can't explain. The fight went on, and I knew I was still in the furnace, but the flames no longer seemed to touch me. It was as though my body had escaped, leaving only my spirit in a fire that had lost its power to torture. Invisible hands seemed to be holding me apart from what was happening, although I was fully conscious of continuing to do my part to help my baby come into the world.

When victory came around midnight, I felt a tear splash on my face as Mike whispered a broken, "Thank God." As I sank into a deep sleep that was almost a coma, I was vaguely wondering why Mike thanked a God he said he didn't believe in.

It was the next day before I knew I had an eight-pound son, perfect in every way except for a sharply pointed head that Mamma assured me, and rightly, would soon round out. It wasn't until I looked at the infant lying in my arms that full realization of that last ten or twelve hours of my ordeal came to me. Then awe filled me, for I knew I had not been alone in my furnace, that another Presence like that a heathen king had once seen walking among flames had been with me.

Of course no mother today would be allowed to go through such a difficult birth as I experienced. Advanced medical skills and x-ray would detect a condition in bone structure indicating the impossibility for a normal birth of an infant as large as I carried. Fifty-nine years ago Caesarean sections were rarely performed in our new state of Oklahoma, where there were few hospitals; in our small town, where there were none, they had probably never been heard of.

Because of this advancement in science and medicine, no mother today is likely to have the spiritual experience that was mine, either. However, I have always been grateful for the physical suffering, for it brought me spiritual freedom. No longer could I doubt that God wanted me to marry Mike and give him the love he had never had. How could I feel otherwise when I looked at our golden-haired little son or listened to his happy chatter? When I recalled the sense of God's presence that had brought me relief while still in tormenting flames?

It was as though God had pronounced a benediction upon my marriage, and in the twenty-four years I was Mike's wife, years filled with insecurity and often turbulence, I never wanted anything else from life than to make him and our children happy.

In the birth of each of the four a miracle was repeated, for my physical handicap did not change. Uremia complicated the birth of our second son, shortening his life-span to two and one-half fear-filled years of anguish, for from the beginning we knew we could not hope to keep him long. The knowledge only made him more precious and us grateful for every day we were allowed in which to pour out love on him.

How great is God when we let him rule our lives! Without his hand on mine I would never have known the maturing experience of being Mike's wife. A spiritual maturing, because our humanity seldom lets us learn to rely on God until every human help fails. That must be why Isaiah calls him "the strength of the poor and needy"; not because he loves the weak ones more, but because they need him more to meet the challenges life offers.

I am thankful, too, that having children was not discouraged when I was young. The high price I paid for each of mine is nothing compared to the happiness they have brought me. Each is a gift from God because they are children of love and God is love.

It is through love that we find true fulfillment, true self-identity, but never freedom—just joy in enslavement.

And our God-relationship is no different. He sets us free through accepting total dependency upon him.

5.

Praise Accents Reality

RECENTLY a beloved friend called by long distance to say she had to undergo surgery to remove a suspicious tumor from her body. "I need your prayers," she said. "Knowing you are praying for me I won't be afraid."

A week later she and her jubilant husband called again to break the good news. The tumor had proved to be nonmalignant. "I can't thank you enough for your prayers," she added fervently.

"Thank God, not me," I told her, thinking it best not to admit that I had not prayed for her as prayer is usually defined. To have done so would have been giving power to evil instead of recognizing the eternal Love that lived within her—her own indwelling Christ. After her first phone call I had thanked God for her faith and left her in his hands, feeling no more concern about her.

Recognition of God as a force of good in our lives is a form of praise. And praise, according to the late Alexis Carrel, is the highest form of prayer. "Prayer," he once wrote, "is an invisible emanation of man's worshiping spirit . . . a force as real as terrestrial gravity."

My friend did not realize it, but she had prayed when she said, "Pray for me." She was recognizing God's power, and that is what counts. The words we speak to him are wholly unimportant. It is the faith in which they are spoken that releases his power and creates miracles. Or that releases the power that keeps us strong in the face of what appears to be trouble.

Another friend once asked me to pray that she be given faith to meet a trial. "Why should I pray for something you already have?" I challenged her." Otherwise, why ask for prayer? Besides, faith is not God's gift to us, it is our gift to him."

Still another friend, so aware of his abiding presence that she cannot withhold her praise of God, sometimes invites skepticism from those who do not understand her enthusiasm. Such was the case when, in need of a car, she suddenly decided against getting a cheap model as discretion dictated she should and instead bought a much more expensive one.

"It is God's gift to me," she kept telling everyone who was interested, declaring the whole transaction to be a miracle. Some of her friends found this amusing, as she had obligated herself to make rather large payments. I was not among those. True, as was pointed out to me, she paid the same price anyone else would have paid, so there seemed no evidence of a miracle.

Yet there had been a miracle. It had taken place when she lost all fear of assuming the heavier indebtedness through the realization that God was not limiting her good. Deep in her heart his voice had spoken, saying, "Fear not," just as truly as he had spoken the same words to Joshua and the children of Israel when they hesitated to go in and possess their promised land. Because my friend associated God with her transaction, continually giving him praise, her purchase proved to be a wise one. Had she depended only upon her human understanding, fear might have raised obstacles that would have prevented her meeting the payments, and she could have lost her investment. Is this not the story of Adam and Eve's lost Eden? They stopped giving God total faith and trouble began.

Praising God serves a dual purpose. It releases the worshiping spirit that brings his power into activity, and it releases our own inner tensions through giving that power reality. And tensions and fear can be a glass wall separating us from God. We may continue to see him in a wholly impersonal and detached way, but until that wall is removed through sincere praise, given freely and joyfully, there is no personal contact. No actual evidence of his great love, for there has been no recognition in our hearts. No faith.

When Jesus entered Jerusalem on a colt and men on the streets went wild with excitement, spreading their garments out as a carpet for him to ride over, shouting praises to God "for all the mighty works that they had seen," some Pharisees in the crowd criticized Jesus for not rebuking his enthusiastic followers. His reply to his critics was, as reported by Luke, ". . . If these should hold their peace, the stones would immediately cry out" (19:40).

God must be praised, he was saying. It is a spiritual law. Without such praise, God ceases to have reality and his power is lost to a needy world. The song of faith must be made.

It is with a warm glow that I recall how a simple song of praise wrought a miracle in my life and, I have never doubted, saved my family from death in a prairie blizzard.

This incident, which came so close to being a tragedy, happened in March of 1923. My husband and I and our two small children were driving from Iowa City to Sioux Falls, South Dakota, when we were overtaken by a late winter storm which had struck with the suddenness typical of weather in the northwest prairie country. From the instant we heard the shrieking of the high wind, so icy cold it seemed to knife right through us, I sensed our very real danger. We drove what was known then as a touring car, with only ill-fitting side curtains for protection. There was no car heater and, except for the six-months-old baby's blanket, only one blanket.

Within half an hour the sky had darkened alarmingly with the heavy snow. My husband had to turn on the car lights, although it was only midafternoon. Not all the snow that filled the air, however, was falling from the sky. Much was being whipped up from dirty mounds piled up on either side of the gravel road by a snow plow after a previous snowstorm, now whirling about in a blinding sheet of white.

The sheet thickened until the car lights were useless. Under the blanket I'd wrapped about the three of us, the children and I shivered violently in spite of our coats and heavy clothing. The road began to fill with drifts through which the car plowed laboriously, and fear was screaming inside me as wildly as was the bitter wind outside.

Although the country was new to us, I had heard about prairie blizzards from my mother, who had been reared on the Kansas plains, and I knew we were caught in one and in very real danger. My husband sensed it, too, and his voice was tense as he said, "Watch out for a house. We'll stop the first chance we have."

Peering hopefully through the isinglass windows of the side curtains for a light or building of any kind, I had the terrifying feeling that we were alone in a vast, empty world of smothering whiteness. Listening to the laboring engine as the car plowed through increasingly high drifts, I tried to think what we could do if it stalled. We would soon freeze in the car, and we had no idea in which direction to start to look for shelter. How far could we go with a six-year-old boy and a baby?

My husband seemed to be reading my thoughts. Worriedly, he said, "Looks like that filling station we passed just before this hit is our best bet. I'll turn around and go back as soon as I can tell where the edge of the road is. We'd get stalled for sure if I tried it along here."

Peering out at the mounds of white, I knew he was right. There was nothing to do but keep moving, hoping for the sight of a farmhouse. Hugging the whimpering children against me for added warmth, I began praying each time I heard the motor miss or a tire start to spin, but it was to the car that I prayed: Don't stop! O please don't stop, or we'll freeze to death!

When it happened we had no warning. The road curved, and then the car stopped with such suddenness I was thrown into the windshield. We had struck what is known in that country as a "draw," where the road bisects a low rolling hill. The short pass had filled with wind-blown snow that reached almost to the radiator cap.

My husband got out of the car, letting in a blast of frigid air that seemed to freeze our breath on our faces. In a moment or so he was reporting, "No chance to go on, but don't worry. I'll back until I can turn around."

But the car seemed unable to go backward either. Hearing that ominous sound of spinning rear wheels, the most profound fear I'd ever known filled me with despair. The thing I had dreaded had happened. How long could we live in this bitter cold?

Letting the motor continue to run, Mike got out again, and I could hear him opening the tool box attached to the running board. It seemed a long time before he got back under the wheel, his gloves stiff with ice, his face blue with cold. He had, he said, dug away enough snow that he should be able to back.

Yet again the engine raced uselessly, with no result but the whining of tortured tires. Again and again, he got in and out, out and in. Filling in the hole the spinning tires had made, first with tools and then with the useless tire chains after they broke under the strain, proved futile. And as fast as he dug away the snow to clear a path behind the car, the wind blew it right back. Soon I saw that his gloves were in ribbons, his hands stiff and fumbling as he shifted gears, and he stumbled as though his feet had lost all feeling.

Having never learned to operate the car, I could not help Mike with that. When I wanted to help shovel snow with my hands, as he'd been doing, he ordered me gruffly to stay in and keep the children warm. The door had been opened so often that the atmosphere inside the car was little different from outside, and I was terrified for them.

With our situation growing more desperate each moment, I became frantic when I saw the gas gauge hovering around the empty mark. Though Mike must have seen it, too, neither of us mentioned it. When he asked for some of the baby's diapers to use as traction, I knew he was making a last stand. But by then I knew it no longer mattered whether or not the wheels turned or spun. There wasn't enough gas to take us anywhere, even if we knew of any place to go.

Yet, as I watched Mike open the door again, getting in painfully slowly, and saw how near he was to complete exhaustion, the deepest love I'd ever known for him filled my heart. He couldn't get out into that wind and whipping snow again! He mustn't! It was better just to give up and sit together, quietly waiting for death. It was comforting to recall that death by freezing was painless—or so I'd heard.

Again the motor raced and the wheels spun uselessly. Mike laid his head down on the wheel, defeat written all over him. Reaching across six-year-old Buddy, I touched my husband's shoulder, speaking far more bravely than I felt. "It's all right, Mike. You can't do anything more."

He muttered hoarsely, "If we only knew which way to start walking . . ."

But we didn't, and we both knew we wouldn't get very far in that howling wind and deep snow. Mike was too exhausted, Buddy too small, and I'd have to carry the baby. Until then I'd been keeping her quiet by nursing her, but that couldn't continue. Although we did not know then how cold it was, we both knew we couldn't survive very long. Later we learned it must have been at least twenty below zero, for it reached thirty-five below that night.

For a moment or so we all sat in silence, giving in to the drowsiness such intense cold brings. Then Buddy woke up and began to cry. "Daddy, I'm cold. Let's get out of here," he whimpered. The baby began to cry, also, and I hadn't the heart to try to quiet her. What did anything matter now?

The children's crying aroused Mike. Reaching for the door handle again, he turned glazed eyes toward me and fairly begged, "Keep them quiet, girl. Sing to them or something."

A rush of pride filled me as he got out again. Mike wasn't going to give up. What did it matter that another effort was useless with that empty gas tank? If he wasn't able to get back in, at least he could die knowing he'd done his best.

My son's shaking voice pulled my thoughts back to him. "Daddy said sing to us, Mommy."

Sing? With my throat in a vise, my tongue so cold and thick it seemed to fill my whole mouth, my lips so stiff I had to force them to move? Then I thought of Mike out in that bitter wind, tortured by the cries of the children he couldn't help, and I knew I had to try. "What shall I sing, Buddy?" It was a question I'd often asked when one of them was ill or needed comforting.

His reply came back. He wanted the familiar Sunday school song I'd been taught as a child and had sung to him so many times. "Sing 'Jesus Loves Me'!" he cried.

Forcing my teeth to stop chattering, I began croaking the familiar words: "Jesus loves me, this I know, For the Bible tells me so. Little ones to him belong . . ." Almost with the first words a picture flashed into my mind, one I'd often seen in my Bible—the picture of Jesus gathering children into his arms. Always the caption used was "Suffer the little children to come unto me."

As suddenly as though I'd heard the words being said, new hope electrified me. How could I have forgotten the love of Jesus for all children? He surely would not let mine die on this snow-covered prairie! I had only to place them in his care and his great love would keep them safe.

The thought warmed me through and through, body as well as spirit. When Mike got back in and fumbled for the gear lever, I reached out again to touch his shoulder. "It will go this time, Mike," I said with conviction, "I know it will," forgetting all about the empty gas tank.

Miraculously, it did. Slowly but surely, the wire wheels with diapers knotted about them to supply traction began to move the car. Mike's face was a mixture of awe and unbelief as he said hoarsely, "We're moving, girl! It can't be, but we are."

He backed until he reached the curve where the wind had made the road seem wider. Then he dared try to turn around, and I could see he was holding his breath as he turned the steering wheel, shifted gears, then turned again, shifting again. But I was no longer afraid, still forgetting to watch the gas gauge, merely relieved that both children slept. My heart, so full of joyous relief that it seemed as though the Jesus the words praised was actually present, was still singing the Sunday school ditty. And when Mike's numb hands fell off the steering wheel and he could not make them obey his will, I reached across Buddy and grabbed the wheel, just as though I'd been told to.

It seems incredulous now that I guided that car with one hand the rest of the way back to that filling station, through drifts that almost blocked the road, against a wind that seemed determined to push us back. I'd never driven a car before, even with two hands, and I was not even under the wheel! My act was automatic, something I could not have done had I thought about it.

Yet I did not feel then (nor do I even now) that it was my hand guiding that car. The Jesus I'd been singing about directed my untrained hand in each movement, and I knew we were going to make it back to help. Strange, too, that I didn't even wonder how the car was getting gas, or how I'd be able to stop it when we reached the station, unable as I was to reach either brake pedal or gear shift.

Later I asked Mike how the car was stopped, and he said he didn't know unless his foot instinctively bore down on the brake pedal. All I know is that we did stop upon reaching the filling station and that I put my hand on the horn and kept it there until the owner came from his living quarters in the rear to give us help.

And such wonderful help! While his wife heated blankets and hot bricks and brought us hot soup, the man was going repeatedly out into the cold to get fresh buckets of snow for Mike's frostbitten hands and feet. All the time he kept talking about how wise we had been not to abandon the car to look for shelter. His was the nearest place and we could never have walked five miles in that storm. Or even one with the children. Men had been known to freeze to death in such blizzards within sight of their homes.

Awe still filled me two days later when the snow plow came through and we made hasty preparations to follow it. There was a slight delay because Mike had to help the station owner push our car about ten feet to a gas pump. It had to be pushed, for the tank was completely empty.

"It beats me," my husband said as we drove away. "That gauge said empty before we got turned around the other day. I know it did."

"I know it too," I admitted. "It was a miracle, Mike." And my husband, who had liked to tease me about my naïve faith when we were first married, had nothing at all to say then.

There can be logical reasons for miracles. In this instance my song of praise to a Christ who loved children had broken the glass wall of fear, lifting my consciousness to meet him in faith. Our safety was assured the instant I accepted it as fact.

Isaiah confirmed this beautiful, comforting truth when he wrote, "Thou meetest him that rejoiceth . . . those that remember Thee in Thy ways" (64:15). *Gratitude*

Meeting God—a miraculous experience, when we remember that all his ways are ways of love. — *His ways are right — Hosea 14:9*

6.

Antidote for Fear

IN TIMES OF danger, to ourselves or our loved ones, God can become very real indeed. Without a power greater than our humanity to turn to, fear could completely defeat, if not destroy us. That is why it was often said during and after World War I that there were no atheists in foxholes.

It is also why the Psalmist David, who knew all about wars, declared, "God is our refuge and strength, a very present help in trouble" (Ps. 46:1). God lacked no reality for him because his God had never failed him in times of danger.

Yet the refuge in which he trusted was intangible, made real only through his faith. And his strength, which enabled him to kill a giant with a single stone and wild beasts with his bare hands, lay in his consciousness of divine help.

God is our refuge and strength. We cant the words and find comfort in them. Yet this truth, like every spiritual truth, carries a condition which if ignored makes the words merely euphemistic phraseology. That condition is contained in the second verse of this beloved forty-sixth Psalm: "Therefore will not we fear."

As great as he is, God cannot be a refuge for the fearful. The very words oppose each other for fear prevents recognition of safety, giving reality only to danger. Because our humanity makes us prone to give substance only to tangible things, we often limit God's power to places or things or circumstances, even means of escape, and are fearful if no such evidence of his care is provided.

Is that not reversing Paul's definition of faith? He says faith must be creative, a substance in itself, not needing proof or substantiation.

The Bible is filled with admonitions to "fear not," emphasizing the spiritual and psychological damage fear can do to us. Abraham was admonished by God to go fearlessly to establish a God-worshiping nation among savage heathen tribes. Suppose he had gone in fear, terrified by the danger about which he had to be fully aware? Could he in that case have become the Father of the Hebrew race? Could God have protected him and directed him without faith on Abraham's part? And faith negates fear or it falls short of being faith.

Moses had to overcome fear, even the fear of his own inadequacy, before he could lead a fearful people to freedom. Joshua's first task as the successor of Moses was to fight fear among the Israelites, camped on the very edge of the land they coveted, but feared to try to possess.

The great prophet Elijah, persecuted by a wicked queen, had every reason to know fear and no doubt did experience it many times, but always lost it in turning to God; Gideon conquered a great host of Midianites with only three hundred fearless men who believed God was directing their leader. Their victory was won by playing upon the fears of their enemies—not by might or power but by stratagem. The story in Judges (7) is interesting and illuminating.

Jesus came to a world living in fear, although civilization had made great advances since the days of Abraham, Moses, Elijah, Gideon and other great ancients whose stories inspire us and give us courage. Although the Israelites of the first century still worshiped the God of their fathers, they lived in constant fear of their conquerors, for theirs was a delicate situation. Although Rome held the reigns of power, she pretended to be a benevolent conqueror as long as Israel paid dearly in exorbitant taxes for the pretense of living as free men.

So then, as now, men lived in fear even as they worshiped God. The rich were afraid to displease their Roman rulers for fear of losing their possessions, if not their lives; the poor feared the rich, and all lived in fear of God, convinced that he would punish them if they broke any of the myriad laws of the synagogue.

In choosing his disciples, Jesus warned them that they must become fearless, even to the point of ignoring religious laws and traditions if service to God or man demanded it. Every lesson he gave them spoke of the power of God, but not a God to fear in the sense they had been taught. The fear they were to feel had the connotation of reverence, a desire to please only through love. Always he emphasized the need of faith on their part to negate fear.

There will be wars to test your faith, he warned them, "but be not terrified . . . and great earthquakes . . . and famines and pestilences and fearful sights . . . they shall lay their hands on you and persecute you, delivering you up to the synagogues and into prisons . . ." (Luke 21:9-12).

Not a very reassuring picture, was it? Yet he added reassurance by saying they were not to fear violence in men or nature, or even in the face of betrayal by those whom they trusted: "For I (the Holy Spirit of God) will give you a mouth and wisdom, which all your adversaries shall not be able to gainsay nor resist . . . there shall not an hair of your head perish" (Luke 21:15-18).

If this was true for those early disciples, is it not true for disciples today? "Jesus Christ, the same yesterday and today and forever," the writer of Hebrews describes him. So what have we to fear if we can develop the faith that Jesus and all the ancient teachers before him tried to instill in believers in God?

Recently I was studying the Apostolic Books from the viewpoint of comparing the human traits of the disciples with ours of today. It was like meeting familiar friends, or like looking into a mirror. The story of a storm on Lake Galilee in which the disciples were caught, as told by Luke (chapter 8) especially amused me, taking me back in time a half century when that same story had saved the lives of myself and my three children—another light for my weak candle of faith. I had read the story the night before a violent storm almost made me forget the Refuge the psalmist sings about, just as those early disciples had forgotten the lessons in faith they had been receiving from Jesus.

The storm on Lake Galilee had been severe enough to arouse natural fears in the disciples, for their ship began to fill with water from the wild waves and it looked as though it might capsize any instant. So they awoke Jesus, who had been quietly sleeping through it all.

In Luke's account we get the impression they awoke their leader to warn him, rather than expecting help. "Master, Master!" we hear them yelling to be heard above the screaming wind and the roar of the sea, "We perish!" No hope of help, just despair.

But Jesus arose and calmed the wind and the sea with a few quiet words. Then he rebuked the disciples. "Where is your faith?" we hear him saying.

Surely there is great significance in that word *where*. Is your faith in God's protective love or in the destructive power of nature? Jesus was asking.

At the time this story proved to be a light for me, we were living in South Dakota, where violent wind and electrical storms were not unusual in late spring and summer. In early spring we had moved from a small upstairs apartment into a roomy house with a large tree-shaded and fenced back yard. There was still snow on the ground the day I found the house, but spring was in the air and spring meant storms. No wonder I was captivated by the sight of an old-fashioned storm cave in one corner of the back yard. It appeared to be well made, with a rounded concrete and tarred roof, cemented walls and floor—the type I'd often seen in Oklahoma. Having been reared in that state, I'd developed an unhealthy fear of storms, and an experience shortly after moving to South Dakota had increased that fear.

That first year we lived in an upstairs flat, and there was one night when I kept the children up until almost morning, fully clothed, expecting a horrible death just any moment. The flat had only an outside stairway, and a violent wind storm had torn down electric wires all over the city, one such cable falling across our stairs. The end lay in the street, spitting fire and leaping about like some fiery-eyed dragon, making a terrifying electrical display. Worse yet, the wire also lay across our roof, and if those flames touched the building we'd be trapped, for we dared not venture down that blocked stairway. The hours seemed endless before overworked electricians got to our area.

I didn't want myself or my family ever to have to live through another such night, so the storm cave was like an answer to prayer. I leased the house, even though it was larger than we actually needed and more rent than we could afford.

My husband and three children shared my enthusiasm about the storm cave. As soon as we were settled in our new home we started cleaning it up and making it ready for use. Before the last of the winter's snow had disappeared, we had a cozy underground shelter, fitted with cots for two-year-old Penny (so-called because of her copper-colored curls) and eight-year-old Buddy; chairs for Mike and myself and fourteen-year-old Sonny; a table and oil lamp and a small cabinet for emergency rations. It looked so inviting the children began anticipating the first storm of the season and I almost lost my dread of it.

My husband was in a neighboring town on business when it struck. Previously we had agreed that in such an event the children and I would go into the cave without delay. So as the ominous-looking cloud began rising rapidly, the roll of thunder filling the air, we made excited preparations to run to our waiting shelter. While Sonny and I closed windows and fastened shutters, Buddy gathered up comic books, cookies, and his and Penny's pajamas, as it was late afternoon. By then the wind was whipping the tree limbs violently, warning us we had no time to lose. Sonny picked up Penny and he and Buddy ran to the back door, yelling at me to hurry.

Halfway across the kitchen, I had an urge to take my Bible with me and finish preparing the Sunday school lesson I'd been working on the night before when I read the account of the storm on Lake Galilee. I dashed back to the living room, but just as I reached out to pick up the Book, words from the story struck me with the impact they must have had on terrified men centuries before. "Where is your faith?"

Where was my faith? In God, or in that ground shelter I'd thanked Him for giving us? If in God, we didn't need any other refuge. Still, the cave was cozy and the kids were excited about going into it, so I picked up the Bible and went back to where the boys waited impatiently, continuing to yell at me to hurry.

Seeing the fear in the eyes of both my sons was like another shock. Had I been instilling unwholesome fears in them instead of courage? Where was my faith, indeed, that I'd had nothing better to offer them than fears?

"We're not going," I heard myself say, although it didn't seem to be my voice saying the words. "I need to study my Sunday school lesson and that oil lamp will give me a headache. Besides, I don't think it's going to be bad."

Buddy began wailing in disappointment but Sonny gave me a sharp look, then set Penny on her feet. "Okay, Mom. If you're not afraid then I'm not either."

Plainly the boy wasn't being strictly honest about that. The memory of that night when we were trapped in an upstairs flat was mirrored in his eyes. But he was ready to battle against fear and I knew I must help him.

Moments later it was too late to change my mind. As if to contradict my words, the storm struck with violent fury. The din made by screaming wind, crashing thunder, rain and hail pounding on the roof mingled with the sound of breaking tree limbs. I was glad when the electricity failed; in the dim light made by the candles Sonny had found it was easier to hide the fear I couldn't quite control. My mind kept tabulating the things that might happen, rehearsing the excuses I'd have to give Mike if disaster struck. He'd been so relieved for us to have the shelter and safety in case he wasn't with us. And with Sonny looking at me so reproachfully it was hard to pretend a cheerfulness I did not feel.

The rain, the first of the season, increased in volume until it became a veritable cloudburst. A kitchen window shutter tore loose, and as the boy helped me mop up water the high wind forced in around the panes, he voiced another fear I'd been fighting. "Do you think Dad's all right?"

"Of course he is," I said hastily. "He's got sense enough to find shelter and wait till the storm is over."

He didn't reply to that but I knew he, like myself, was thinking of how far apart shelters were on that highway, and of the danger of falling tree limbs—the same danger we were in because I hadn't had sense enough to use the shelter we'd prepared.

Then again I seemed to hear a stern, challenging voice: *Where is your faith?* And suddenly complete peace was mine. "Daddy's all right," I told my worried son, and this time my voice carried conviction, "and so are we. God can take as good care of all of us in one place as another."

The confidence in my voice made him visibly relax. "Hey, why don't we play some checkers while we wait? Bet I can beat you."

"You're on," I said, an odd relief making my voice gay.

The checker tournament was still going on, with me losing, when Mike came in. He'd waited out the storm in a filling station fifteen miles away and had found driving slow and hazardous afterward because of tree limbs, electric wires, and other debris littering the highway and city streets.

"I wasn't worried about you," he said reproachfully. "I was sure you'd go to the cave. Didn't you have warning enough?"

"We had time enough," I admitted. "I just decided we shouldn't go."

Mike was half angry, half amused. "I don't get it," he kept saying. "We rent a house bigger than we need because it has a storm cave, we buy stuff to fix it up, then you sit out one of the worst storms in years, from what I hear, risking the kids' lives when you could have been safe. I sure don't get it."

"It was just a hunch," I said. What else could I say to a man who found it difficult to share my erratic faith?

The next morning while I prepared breakfast Mike and Sonny went into the back yard to check on damage done to trees and flowers. They came back in looking as though they'd received a shock. Mike's voice shook a little as he told me what they had found. Across the wooden door to our storm cave a heavy tree limb lay. After he and Sonny had moved it, they'd opened the cellar door on an impulse, then stared in stunned surprise at the sight that met their eyes. Water completely filled our shelter, almost reaching the top step, with cots and tables and chairs floating against the roof.

"It's a good thing you had a hunch not to go," he added, fervently. "You'd have all been trapped in there for you never could have raised that door against the wind and with that limb across it."

He was visibly shaken at the thought of our narrow escape, just as I was. But in my heart I knew, and I felt he did too, that my "hunch" had to be another miracle. The challenge to my faith, an echo of words spoken centuries before, came from something beyond my humanity.

If I'd had any doubts about that, they would have been resolved by another incident that happened six weeks later. When Mike's vacation time came we decided to drive into North Dakota to see the historic Badlands and other points of interest in the state. Because today's comfortable motels were unknown in that country at that time, we carried camping equipment and supplies, stopping whenever and wherever the fancy struck us.

It was while we were crossing the bald prairies that make up a large part of the state that the car's engine began missing. Sighting the roofs of a small town in the distance, Mike turned in at a ball park. We'd make camp for the rest of the day and night, he decided, and have the car worked on. As soon as he and Sonny had our floored tent up he drove away in search of a mechanic.

For a while the boys amused themselves playing on some wooden bleachers about a hundred feet from our tent. Then a sudden rain storm sent them running back to share the tent with Penny and me. The rain was heavy but unaccompanied by wind and stopped as suddenly as it had begun. Quickly the air became stifling in the steamy tent, so the boys suggested we all go sit on the bleachers.

The instant we stepped outside, however, Sonny gave a frightened shout: "Look, Mom! Look what's coming!"

It was the most terrifying sight I'd ever seen—a huge gray-green cloud that seemed to be rolling along the prairie toward us. As we stared it lifted and we could see it was almost perfectly funnel-shaped. Although I'd never actually seen a tornado I knew I was looking at one then. And looking at death, for the small end of the funnel seemed to be dragging along the ground, writhing and twisting like a blacksnake wielded by a giant hand.

Petrified with terror, hardly able to breathe in the smothering closeness of the air, we watched that writhing tail pick up a building we could barely see in the distance, lift it off the ground, then drop it in scattering pieces.

"What'll we do?" my son cried, fear throbbing in his voice. "It's coming this way!"

What could we do? We stood on a bald prairie beside a canvas tent. The wooden bleachers flashed into my mind, but before I could speak something stopped me. Not a voice, not even a connected thought. Just a verse of Scripture: "Be still and know that I am God."

It acted like a strong sedative. My fear was gone and I heard myself speaking calmly and naturally. "We won't do anything, just stand here and watch. God will take care of us, like he did about the storm cellar."

Thinking back on it later, I couldn't even feel sure I'd said those words, I felt so completely detatched as I stood there with my children watching death roaring toward us, I'm sure they felt the same way, for there wasn't a sound from any of them, not even a whimper from Penny, as the wind became a deafening roar. Then with a swoosh that seemed to suck the very breath from our lungs the monster lifted and roared over us, then reached down that tail again to pick up the bleachers, turning them into kindling wood.

Be still. I knew then why that particular verse had flashed into my mind to stop us from running right into the path of destruction. Of course I know that all the rules say we should have lain flat on the ground, but there hadn't been time—nor necessity—to think of that right then. No necessity, for I had turned to God.

The next day we drove past the wreckage of the farm house we'd seen destroyed. The tragic scene of devastation still lives vividly in memory. Two people had been killed. Only the floor of the house was left intact. Standing in the place where a kitchen had been was a wood range, untouched, the stovepipe sticking up into empty space where a chimney had been. Tornadic winds do freakish things like that and men can't explain them. Such things are not acts of God, but results of the laws of physics.

Looking in awe at that unsupported stovepipe, I saw myself and my children protected in the midst of devastation, and words of the psalmist flashed into my mind: "God is our refuge" (46:1).

God, our refuge—not man-made devices that can fail when most needed. God, all-wise, all-loving, knowing every need before we turn to him for protection and help.

"There is a river," verse four of this beautiful psalm reads, "the streams whereof shall make glad the city of God, the holy place of the tabernacles of the Most High."

This city of God, the holy place, can only be within ourselves, since Jesus is our authority that "the Kingdom of God is within you." The river is the stream of conscious awareness of that God dwelling with us, guaranteeing safety so long as the stream is free-flowing, not clogged with fears or mental reservations.

"Therefore will not we fear," David sings so confidently, "though the earth be removed and though the mountains be carried into the midst of the sea" (v. 2). Was that a message only for his day, or is it still valid for us in today's uncertain world?

Meteorologists tell us that in the center of every hurricane is an area of calmness known as the eye of the storm. In the center of all life's storms I see God as the Eye where, through faith, we can find stillness and peace, even as the rest of the world is battered and bruised by violence in man or nature. *Praise God!*

This time-honored refuge has never failed men.

7.

The Eternal Presence

ONLY RECENTLY a letter came from a widowed friend, telling me her only son had been killed in Viet Nam. My heart ached for her in her loss, but her despairing words aroused even deeper compassion.

"I prayed so hard for his safety," she wrote, "and I can't understand why God didn't answer my prayers. I've always had faith in him. How could he leave me alone like this?"

Her poignant cry carried me back thirty-five years to my own Gethsemane, when I had to learn that there is a fine line between faith and trust. We may have faith and still arbitrarily dictate to God instead of accepting his will in our lives, as did Jesus in his night of Gethsemane. It is not enough to believe in God's greatness unless we believe in his love; it is not enough to believe in his love unless we give him love in return. Love without trust is only a temporary emotion.

What could I say to comfort my heartbroken friend? Words can seem so trite, so futile, at such times as this. Human words, that is, but not God's words, preserved for us through eons of time. So I wrote her what my heart dictated: "Read Psalm 139, especially verses eight to ten; and I pray they speak to you what they once said to me when I felt abandoned and alone—the truth that God never leaves us alone if we put our trust in him."

After closing the letter, I still felt there was too much left unsaid, so I opened my Bible and read this psalm of David again where he wrote, ". . . Whither shall I flee from thy presence? If I ascend up into heaven, thou art there: if I make my bed in hell, behold, thou art there. If I take the wings of the morning, and dwell in the uttermost parts of the sea; Even there shall thy hand lead me, and thy right hand shall hold me" (139:7–10).

Much, much more than beautiful words—they are beautiful, beautiful truth. Who could know that better than I? So again I relive the time I made my bed in hell and found God there, just as I'd found him when I soared "on the wings of the morning." I pray that the telling of it may say to my friend and countless others sharing her hours of desolation how truly dependable God is "when the darkness shall cover me"; how "even the night shall be light about me," for "the darkness and the light are both alike to thee."

The tragic period in our national history known as the Great Depression threw millions of believers in God into darkness. My own black period began when my husband suffered a serious heart attack while struggling to make a new beginning in Oklahoma after the failure of banks all over South Dakota had left us penniless and him jobless.

The heart attack hospitalized Mike for three months and left him completely incapacitated. For four bitterly hard years, the boys and I managed to get along by sharing my parents' home and denying ourselves everything that makes life enjoyable. As Mike began slowly to improve, we dared hope the doctor was right when he suggested the dry climate of Arizona might offer Mike a new lease on life. For many years he had suffered from bronchial asthma, which continued to be a strain on his weakened heart. If that could be relieved, he might have a chance to live a nearly normal life.

Just the hope of making the move so revived Mike's spirits that I was determined to try it. After learning there was a large Veterans Hospital in Tucson, Arizona, which Mike would be eligible to enter if he suffered another attack, since he had enlisted at the age of eighteen and had served two years in the Philippines during the Spanish–American war, I was more determined than ever. We had started making excited plans when we suffered another blow. The pension of sixty dollars a month which Mike had been receiving since his illness was suddenly cut off by presidential edict, as were all pensions granted within the five-year period prior to that date. A move regarded to be in the interests of national economy looked like a death knell to our hopes.

The disappointment brought on another attack for Mike. In my fear I recklessly promised him we'd go, anyway, as soon as he was able. By then the possibility had become an opium dream with me as well as with him, for I wanted nothing in the world as much as to see my husband well again and able to reassume responsibilities I felt I could no longer carry on. Our oldest son had married a lovely girl the year before. They were expecting a child in a few months and I wanted terribly to free him to live his own life. Also I felt we'd imposed much too long on my aging parents, who had only a very limited income for themselves.

From this vantage point of time I can see that it was desperation, not faith, that made me start out that autumn day with a gravely ill husband, a sixteen-year-old boy, and a ten-year-old girl dependent upon me, with all our possessions stacked in a five-year-old Ford and less than three hundred dollars in my purse—all my family and I had been able to raise. Between us, Buddy and I could manage until Mike was well again, I'd assured my worried parents and son so often I began to believe it myself.

An impractical dream—but dreams can sustain the spirit when there is nothing else to hold to. Living with the constant fear that every asthma attack would be too much for Mike's weakened heart, I had lost sight of the fact that God could or would lighten my burdens. The fight for survival engrossed our every thought, to the extent that I couldn't care too deeply that Buddy had to drop out of high school in his senior year. All of America, it seemed, had quit living for tomorrow. Only today mattered.

Even though I wasn't consciously aware of the Eternal Presence, I know he made that long trip with us. How else could Mike have endured it so well, almost his old relaxed, laughing self? And how else could things have gone so smoothly all the way that we felt absolutely triumphant when we sighted what we took to be our "Promised Land," sitting in the warm desert sun like a dozing Indian squaw?

Possessing our Canaan, we soon found out, was a different story. The cheapest place we could find to live in was a tourist court within a mile or so of the hospital. A cabin there, as such lodgings were called then, consisting of two sparsely furnished, comfortless rooms, rented for five dollars a week—an enormous sum for us to pay right then.

Yet the higher altitude and its clear, dry air was just what Mike needed, we told ourselves happily. After a week's rest he felt so well he insisted upon looking for work. The resulting collapse put him back in bed and called for the expenses of a doctor, who ordered him to stay there indefinitely. The doctor recommended hospitalization, but I quickly learned that red tape would have to be cut in Washington and that would take time.

That meant no school for Penny, either. She had to be nurse for her father while Buddy and I spent every day looking for work—any kind of work, just so we could have the bare necessities and buy the medicine Mike had to have. That became a hopeless, weary search. The town seemed filled with health-seekers and their families, many as destitute as we were, all wanting work.

Suddenly the Depression, which had been a crisis to be lived through, became a horrible, threatening enemy, a giant octopus with thousands of legs and arms and hopeless faces. We felt ourselves to be a part of its repulsive body. In spite of all the care I exercised, our money vanished alarmingly fast. Soon we dared not buy gas, but walked the streets in our useless search. Every moment I was away from my sick husband, left to the sole care of a ten-year-old child, was an agony. And every time I returned to face his hopeful, questioning eyes, was worse. Worry and fear were taking their toll from Mike, I knew, but it was impossible to hide our situation from him.

Help from welfare agencies, of the kind that is available today was denied non-residents, and the few bread lines there were always ran out of food with long lines still waiting. The day I reached the hard, hard decision to ask Sonny to send us help I received a letter from him, saying his pregnant wife had been sick and that my father was far from well and worrying greatly about us. The filling station where Sonny had been working had changed hands and he'd been out of a job for weeks. Fortunately, he had just been employed at a grocery store at ten dollars a week. How could I add to his burdens and my parents' worry? We'd keep trying, Buddy and I decided after he found a market in the neighborhood that would give him an hour or so of work each day in exchange for staples.

When we give reality to hunger and need such as we faced, God becomes very unreal—forgotten. Such is the weak link in our faith, and such is the power in the law of acceptance. Only what our minds accept has reality, and the day I heard the YWCA had opened a registry office to take applications for jobs they would do what they could to obtain, my mind was accepting total defeat. Our money was gone and we faced actual hunger; Mike needed the digitalis that kept his heart action normal, and every effort Buddy and I had made to sell our old car for any price had failed. Rent on our cabin was due, and I did not know how much longer we'd be allowed to stay at the court.

It was after a sleepless night and without any breakfast that I walked almost two miles to apply to the YWCA for help. Although I arrived shortly after eight, I was stunned to see that the line in front of the building was almost two blocks long. Nevertheless, I joined it, and until well after noon I became a part of a human chain that moved so slowly progress seemed undetectable.

During those long hours, Job had nothing on me when it came to self-pity. Faint with hunger and the heat of the desert sun, sick with the need of body elimination and yet not daring to leave my place in the slowly moving line, I felt completely separated from all good and ready to accept the status of beggars for myself and my family.

When I did finally get inside and to a registration desk, I was at the point of complete exhaustion. A tired-looking young woman had nothing but more discouragement to offer me, however, after questioning me about my qualifications. I'd taught school in Oklahoma but had no Arizona certificate; I'd written some feature articles for the South Dakota newspaper on which Mike worked before it went bankrupt and had often helped him with his copy, but I'd never learned to type. He had always done that. I had clerked in stores for short periods of time and felt confident I could hold down a job like that.

She shook her head wearily, pointing to the long lists on her desk. There were over fifty experienced clerks and several qualified teachers and typists asking for jobs, and no newspaper writers were wanted. All those ahead of me would have to be considered first, and it might take weeks, even months, to place them.

"I'll try anything," I said desperately, but her reply to that was, "So would most of these. I'll take your name and phone number but I can't promise you anything. My advice is to go back to Oklahoma."

Go back? She made it sound so easy. But we had no money for gas or food, and my husband was too sick to travel. Right then there seemed to be no way of staying, either, but I left the telephone number of the tourist court, wondering as I did so where we would be by the time such a call ever came. We couldn't stay there much longer without rent money.

I trudged wearily back to the court, too tired even to think and almost beyond the point of feeling. There was nothing but despair in my heart as I finally reached our cabin. Opening the door, I stopped, staring with something close to shock at a crude poster Penny had made from a sheet of drawing paper and tacked on the wall. "Trust in God and He will help," she had printed in bold letters.

The challenging words awakened me rudely. For so long I'd been too worried, too distraught, even to pray. Too afraid. Our problems seemed so big, and without answers. Could God make work where there wasn't any? And work was what we had to have.

I took down the poster and carried it into the room where Mike lay so white and lifeless. Tears filled his eyes as he looked at it, but his words were another shock. "Maybe you have been overlooking a bet, girl."

That from Mike, who had never even pretended any interest in religion! Now he and a worried child were having to remind me that my faith had been small when it needed to be big. Shame flooded me, but suddenly my heart was lighter.

Just then Buddy came in with a sack of potatoes with which he'd been paid for splitting old boards into bundles of kindling to sell to campers on the desert. There were many living like that, some for their health's sake, others for the sake of economy. As I prepared the potatoes for supper, I recalled that I'd entertained the idea of our trying that mode of living when, and if, I could get Mike into the hospital. Now, suddenly, I didn't feel we'd be reduced to that.

Penny had reminded me that we were not wholly alone in this alien land. We still had God with us and we still had food. Boiled potatoes, even without butter, can be a feast when one is really hungry, and we feasted that night.

After the others were asleep that night, I dug around and found my neglected Bible, opening it to the Psalms, always a favorite of mine. It seemed entirely by accident that I found myself reading the 139th: "O Lord, thou hast searched me, and known me. Thou knowest my downsitting and mine uprising; thou understandest my thought afar off" (vv. 1–2).

I couldn't read any further for the hot tears blinding my eyes. It was as though a living Presence stood beside me saying those comforting words, Someone who understood all I'd been through and what I was facing now; who could forgive all my mistakes, my "downsittings" because he knew every thought.

Blinking away the tears, I read on: "If I ascend up into heaven, thou art there: if I make my bed in hell, behold, thou art there" (v. 8). So I wasn't alone, as I'd been thinking. That meant there was an answer to our problems and an understanding God would help me find it.

Turning back to Exodus, I read again of how God fed the wandering Israelites, and it was almost as though I was reading the story for the first time. It had a new impact, for I was no longer reading about people who lived in the dim past. My family and I were the homeless wanderers, ours the hunger and the need; my child was the Moses declaring faith in a living God that cared about people, and I was the repentant heart ready to believe. When I closed the Bible and went to bed it was to fall asleep at once, every burden lifted from my shoulders by the one who shared my "hell."

The next morning I was about to leave the house when the court manager called me to the telephone. It was the registration clerk at the YW, saying she had a job for me if I would consider it. A winter visitor who had broken her arm the week before wanted to leave the hospital and return to her apartment if she could find a reliable woman to be nurse, cook, and housekeeper. "I know this is not the kind of work you are looking for," the clerk added, almost apologetically, "but I haven't any on my list that I feel would please her, except possibly you."

"I'll take it," I said without hesitation, never doubting it was my answer from God. Ten dollars a week, my meals, and the privilege of sleeping at home! Who else but God could have worked such magic? And to make it perfect, the woman herself suggested she pay me by the day, making it possible for me to buy gas and drive across town. What did it matter that it was menial work I would once have scorned doing? It had come from God, and that was enough.

Yet even more "manna" was to be sent us. The grocery where Buddy had been doing odd chores gave him steady employment at fifty cents a day, plus wood for our small heater. A week later came the wonderful news that Mike was being admitted to the government hospital. And they would even send an ambulance for him!

The night after that news came, I looked up the comforting Psalm again, my heart fairly singing as I read, "If I take the wings of the morning . . . even there shalt thy hand lead me and thy right hand shall hold me" (v. 9–10). It was so comforting, so good, to know I was being led instead of having to wander around alone, lost and afraid.

If there are any reading this who feel I was limiting God's power by seeing my lowly job as coming from him, I can only say that he gave me much, much more than a job—more than I knew then I was receiving. He gave me a new experience, which is always broadening, and needed lessons in humility and patience. He lifted me above self-pity when I ate alone in a stranger's kitchen, entered the building by the back door, and gratefully accepted leftover food and discarded clothing for the sake of my children. And he gave me a friend before my two months of employment ended.

He gave me also a new sense of values, because I learned that one can take pride in doing anything well, even when it is only cleaning another's stove or bathtub. But more than all else, God gave me a deepening compassion for all unfortunates. Driving past lines of job-seekers or groups of hopeless-looking men on my way to work each morning, I longed to stop and tell them all that God cared about their plight. Hadn't he proven that to me?

Two months later, however, sitting in the office of the hospital supervisor, listening to words that pierced my heart like sharp arrows, I felt the black, lonely darkness closing in on me again. Mike was going to die! The battle to possess our new world was over. He'd suffered an occlusion; the clot had lodged in his lungs and was not dissolving. They gave him two weeks, possibly less, to live.

"You should notify his son in Oklahoma," the doctor had added, but by then I was walking out, too dazed with shock to think or even feel. It was as though I were walking off into space, with nothing under my feet, no substance with reality to hold to.

I was still in that state of shock when I had to break the news to Mike's children. "The doctor says we should let Sonny know," I added hopelessly, "but there's no use telling him yet. There's nothing he could do. I don't know what we're going to do, either. I just don't know."

Penny had wiped away tears with the back of her hand as she said, staunchly, "I bet God knows."

Her reminder that we were not alone in this black hour made me feel as though invisible, tender and strong arms had been laid about my shoulders.

Buddy got up and walked out, the pain in his eyes making me forget my own grief; yet I understood that he had to be alone, so I didn't follow him.

After Penny had quietly cried herself to sleep, I opened my Bible and again read the comforting assurance that I did not have to face this cataclysmic experience alone—"Though I make my bed in hell, thou art there."

The tears came then, washing away some of the terrible aloneness and fear engulfing me. "Stay with me in this hell, Lord God," I whispered, "and I won't be afraid."

The darkness had lifted enough by the time I went back to the hospital the next day that I was able to obey the doctor's stern orders not to betray Mike's condition to him. I even managed to tease him about being given a private room. "You must be using your charm on the nurses, Mike."

"Could be," he said, with a laugh that cut me to the quick. "I must be getting back my sex appeal, the way they argue about which one gets to shave me and comb my hair."

He added, the laughter leaving his eyes, "They really have been swell. I guess I might as well tell you now that I had a rough time a couple of weeks ago. I made them promise not to tell you because I didn't want you worrying about me. But I'm about okay again now."

I had to make an excuse to hurry away, for I couldn't hold back the hot tears burning my eyelids any longer. As I drove back to the court, half blinded by the scalding moisture, I kept whispering his words, over and over. "You're okay, Mike—you're okay, for you have God with you, too. I know you do."

Upon reaching the little place we were calling home, I found another evidence of God's presence. It was in the form of a telegram from my father which read, "Sonny is on his way to you. God bless and comfort you."

"But how did they know?" I asked. "Buddy, did you . . . ?"

"I wired him last night," my son admitted. "I knew he'd find a way to come."

Shame flooded me. Why hadn't I had that much faith?

The next morning, seeing the longing in Buddy's eyes, I told him to go tell his employer he wouldn't be working for a while, then come back and go to the hospital with me. Even though I was again jobless, my employer having returned to her home in the East the week before, and our total assets with which to meet this crisis amounted to less than ten dollars, I felt almost light-hearted over my decision for both of us to spend all the time left us with Mike. What came after there was no more time I'd leave with God.

It was late that afternoon when we left the hospital to go home to see about Penny (who wasn't permitted to visit the hospital because she was under twelve) and prepare some supper. We hadn't eaten since morning. Upon walking into the kitchen, we found the table loaded with food—hot dishes, a cake, fruit. The news about Mike had spread through the court, and my neighbors, strangers with whom I'd barely exchanged greetings, had shown their sympathy in this way.

That was only the beginning. They had told Penny to tell me there would be food every day as long as we had to stay at the hospital. Later that evening the court manager came over to tell me not to worry about the weekly rent, about due. It could wait. And the next morning the owner of the filling station where we bought gas offered us unlimited credit so that we could make the trips back and forth to the hospital.

God was expressing himself through human hearts. Do we need any more proof that he has his habitation in man? The love my children and I received from strangers during those trying days made God as real as though he literally walked beside me, holding my hand. And with my children, for three days later Sonny was there, having hitchhiked his way in order to bring with him money he knew I must need desperately.

A few days later Mike was gone, too suddenly to have reality. Although breathing heavily, he had laughed and joked with the boys the night before, but when we reached the hospital that morning we found a nurse stripping his bed. "He's gone," she said simply, and handed me his hat and empty wallet. Like a zombie I accepted them and went outside to sit on a bench in the sun while the boys talked to the supervisor.

He's gone . . . he's gone . . . The nurse's words kept beating in my brain like harsh drums as I sat there, clutching all that was left of Mike. *Gone . . .* but gone where? He couldn't just disappear, suddenly become nothing. We'd have to bury his body, once so vital and strong and pulsing with love, as though it had turned into something repulsive. But what about his brilliant mind, the generous and loving spirit that had made him Mike? What about his easy laughter, the lightning flashes of temper, the ambitious dreams that never saw realization? All that had been Mike, too. Could they just suddenly become nothing?

I don't know, a despairing voice inside me answered. *I don't know where Mike is or what I'm going to do now. I don't even know how we're going to do the things for him that still have to be done. I hope you know, God. Penny says you do.*

He knew. Twenty-four hours later Penny and I were on a train speeding toward Oklahoma, with Mike riding in a flag-draped casket in the express car ahead of us. And somewhere on a highway his sons were driving the old car with its slick tires, carrying barely enough money to buy gas en route, but with food given by generous neighbors. But what would they do if a tire blew out or the old engine developed trouble? "Don't worry, Mom," Mike's sons had said to me when they left a few hours ahead of my train. "We'll be there almost as soon as you."

Strangely enough (or was it strange?), I didn't worry about them. God was a living presence who had been looking after us wonderfully, smoothing out all the rough, impassable places. The government, we'd found, would pay for the cost of taking Mike back to the cemetery where we had a family plot and for my fare to accompany him. My parents needed and wanted us, and Sonny's expectant wife and his job were waiting for him.

Although it was a grieving, seemingly defeated woman who made that return trip at the expense of a benevolent government, she was a stronger, more mature one than when she'd left Oklahoma a few months before. This woman, desolate as she was over separation from the most important person in her world, felt less alone than the other one, because deep in her heart a new faith had been born and God given a new reality.

8.
A Mighty Voice

WHEN THOMAS EDISON, modern miracle-worker, was asked the secret of his inventive powers, he is said to have replied, "I listen within."

Surely this is the secret that is filling our world with miracles today, and the secret that brought about many of the miracles of Bible times. The Divine Voice within dictates and directs. But as the ancients acknowledged, it is not always recognized as belonging to God.

One of the most significant things President Richard Nixon said in his inaugural speech was that we needed to stop shouting at each other in order to be able to talk over solutions to national problems. This same attitude can be applied to our God-relationship. How can we hear him directing us until we quiet the clamoring voices of fear? Until we stop listening to complaints of our bodies and "listen within" to the still small voice of love?

Throughout the Bible, especially in the Old Testament and Psalms, we read repeated references to the voice of God, often giving specific directions about human problems. All evidence supports the belief that this was rarely, if ever, an audible voice, but heard only by the one to whom God spoke, a fact that made it none the less real.

In 1 Kings 19 we read a vivid description of how God, a Spirit without form, speaks to men. When the prophet Elijah went into hiding on Mt. Horeb to escape the vengeful wrath of the wicked queen Jezebel, "the word of the Lord came to him," asking what he was doing there. How that word was given we are not told, but it must have been from within his own consciousness. In any case, Elijah's reaction was much as yours or mine might have been. He proceeded to tell the Lord God all his troubles in detail, just as though God didn't already know, having warned Elijah to flee from the queen. How often we mortals use precious prayer moments to inform God, instead of letting him inform us.

Then Elijah was given a demonstration that helps our own understanding. A strong wind arose, breaking rocks upon the mountainside, but "the Lord was not in the wind." An earthquake followed, and we can imagine the uproar that created, "but the Lord was not in the earthquake." A fire followed that, flames crackling and roaring, but it was still not the voice the prophet was listening for.

Finally, however, he heard it—just "a still small voice." But he recognized it, and such awe filled him that he hid his face in his mantle. And when the question was repeated, "What doest thou here, Elijah?," we can be sure his answer sounded different, even though he used the same words, for this time he received the instructions he'd been waiting to hear, to return to Damascus to anoint a new king for Syria.

Quietness and confidence had established communication, where sound and fury could not. If this was true for Elijah, is it not true for us today? And without communication with God, how can there be divine direction?

There can be many ways of establishing this communication, but the psalmist sums them all up where he says, "He doth send out his voice, and that a mighty voice" (68:33).

Mighty, but not always loud or spectacular. Mighty in power to demonstrate his eternal love when we can still the clamoring voices of the world in order to hear him.

A remarkable, although not dramatic, demonstration of this truth was given me during World War II. At the time my eighty-two-year-old mother and I were living alone in the family home, several years after my father's death. My two married sons had enlisted in the service and were stationed overseas; Penny had recently married and was living near her husband's Air Force training base.

During those troubled war years, God seemed less real than he should. We were all so surrounded with fear and negativity that it was hard to still our minds enough to feel his presence. Patriotism was so aroused in all of us that we regressed to the attitude of the ancient Israelites and limited our prayers to asking protection for our loved ones and our country, forgetting the universality of the God to whom we prayed.

Like millions of other mothers, I was caught in a vortex of maternal fears, but my job as society editor and columnist for the local newspaper and my church activities helped me keep my emotional balance. It wasn't until my mother, always active and mentally alert, began suddenly to fail that I felt myself slipping.

Like most small towns, ours had been robbed of doctors by the war, except for one young, inexperienced, overworked one. He could find no apparent reason for the pain my ill mother insisted she suffered, pain that made her cry and often scream for hours every night. Convinced it must all be in her mind, he told us we must deny her the small relief she'd been receiving from the codeine tablets he'd allowed her. There was great danger of addiction with the elderly, he warned.

Too soon to realize what was happening, I found myself living with a stranger. She had my mother's face, but she wasn't the quiet, reserved, uncomplaining woman I'd always known. Instead, she became querulous and demanding, wanting more attention than I had time to give her, in spite of my deep concern about her.

When she began showing definite signs of mental confusion at unexpected times, I became afraid to leave her alone. The only solution I could find was to do all my office and telephone work at home, as well as to take over the housework she had always delighted in doing.

This, too, she made extremely difficult for me except during the hours she slept, and every napping hour meant wakefulness when night came. Very soon the nights became unbearable, with little or no sleep for either of us. If Mamma wasn't screaming and moaning, she was restless, getting in and out of bed and often falling. It got to where I dared not leave her, yet could get no rest if I stayed in the room with her. The strain began draining my strength, but my desperate efforts to get help, either at the office or at home, failed.

For one thing, since my job was future as well as present subsistence, I felt I had to keep it. For another, my mother, who had always been reserved, almost to the point of being anti-social, developed a violent antipathy toward having anyone but me around her. Early in her illness she'd extracted the promise from me that I would not take her to a hospital; in fact, the mere word so disturbed her that I'd never brought it up. Then when I reached the point of desperation and consulted her doctor about hospitalization for her, he said it was impossible. Our small local hospital was overcrowded and understaffed, and my mother's type of illness would call for more attention than she could be given. Besides, to take her against her will might be very injurious.

As her condition worsened, I knew I had to have help or break down under the strain myself. Yet I couldn't bring myself to ask Penny to leave her husband, who was due to sail in a few weeks. Suppose he never came back? Both my daughters-in-law lived in distant states and had small children; one of my brothers was an invalid needing constant care, and another brother was involved in important defense work in Oklahoma City; both my sisters had husbands in the service and were involved in defense work themselves.

There was no one I felt I could call upon that Mamma would tolerate. Also I felt strongly that caring for her myself was my job and mine alone. Hadn't she cared for my children when I was unable to? And for me when I was homeless and sick in spirit? And Mike? Now she leaned on me and I couldn't fail her, even though it meant struggling under a load too heavy to carry alone.

Yet not entirely alone. A little fox terrier I was keeping for a soldier made those days and nights of double duty, when I dared not let Mamma out of my sight, endurable. And for a while made it possible for me to snatch an hour or so of sleep each night.

Spot was superhuman in understanding, and I drafted him into acting as substitute nurse at night, for Mamma loved him also. By putting his bed beside hers and teaching him to wake me if she tried to get up, I dared go across the hall to my own room where her cries reached me only faintly and I could sleep from sheer exhaustion. The instant Mamma started to get out of bed, Spot would run in and jump up on my bed, tugging at the covers until I came fully awake.

After he awakened me one night and I ran in to find Mamma

on the floor, barely conscious, I knew she mustn't be left with just Spot any more, so I put a cot in the room with her. Then there was no rest at all for me. After several nights of listening to her continuous moaning and crying I felt I was very near the breaking point myself.

The day I discovered that the sedative pills I'd carefully hidden from her were gone I touched bottom. She had, I realized, found them while I was on one of my brief trips to the newspaper with copy. But when? And how many capsules had been in the box, now empty? I couldn't recall, but I was terrified. Were what she'd taken responsible for her increased suffering? I knew nothing at all about drug addiction or its indications. All I knew was that I had to have help with Mamma, that the help I'd tried to give her wasn't enough.

But where? How? Even if it were possible to get her into the hospital, dare I force her to go? Much of the time she was rational, even if erratic, and I couldn't bear the thought of her feeling deserted, left to the care of strangers. I owed her so much love. So very much.

That night I lay on my cot, sleepless, despairing, as Mamma moaned and cried aloud by turns. Over and over I tried to formulate some plan for getting help for both of us, but my mind seemed incapable of thought. To call on friends for even temporary relief seemed intolerable. Mamma, who had never before given in to illness, had a right to privacy in her hours of defeat, or so it seemed to me; yet I had to do more for her than I'd done.

As though completely understanding my mental anguish, Spot came over to lick my hands, whining softly. Childishly I whispered, "What can we do, Spot? We both love her. How can we help her?"

Standing on his hind legs, he crossed his front paws on the edge of my cot, resting his head on them, eyes closed. The resemblance to an attitude of prayer was startling. "Why, Spot," I exclaimed, "are you saying a prayer for her?"

Then it struck me like a blow. Why hadn't I been asking God for help instead of looking for answers myself? He loved my mother, too. I'd forgotten how often I'd seen his great love demonstrated in miraculous ways.

Resting my hand on Spot's head, I prayed then, no longer from a despairing heart but from a hopeful one, and felt that a little dumb animal prayed with me: *Tell us how we can help her, Lord Jesus. Show us what to do.*

Almost as I whispered the words I fell asleep. I hadn't meant to, but exhaustion claimed me—or was it peace? An hour or so later I woke with a start, realizing that it was dawn and that Mamma also slept quietly, as though my peace had touched her. Then what had awakened me?

A voice, I realized instantly. A voice had been saying, "Take her to Oklahoma City. There'll be room in a hospital there."

It had to be a dream, for it didn't make sense. According to the papers and things I'd heard, the Oklahoma City hospitals were as crowded and understaffed as our small one. It would require a priority rating to get an out-of-town patient into one, and I didn't even know the name of a doctor there. And hadn't Mamma made me promise not to hospitalize her? Not only that, she wasn't able to make that sixty-mile drive. Even if I could get the gas ration, I wouldn't dare start with her.

Yet as I got up and wearily began the day's activities, I couldn't dismiss that voice. It kept ringing in my ears while, with Mamma still asleep, I went to the telephone and awoke our local physician, timidly asking him if he thought there was any chance of getting her admitted to an Oklahoma City hospital. He was kind, but discouraging. No chance at all, he declared. He'd tried only a few days before but had failed to get another patient in. Besides, he didn't regard Mamma as an emergency case. In his opinion she could live months, or even years. If I wanted to consider the state mental institution . . .

I didn't, I said almost violently. My mother was perfectly normal most of the time and I couldn't do that to her. After breaking the connection, I sat at my desk, forcing my mind to be still, and again I heard, like an echo, the words ringing in my ears. *Take her to Oklahoma City.*

My doubts began to dissolve. If the words were in answer to my prayer, then God would open doors. He wouldn't tell me to try the impossible. So while I coaxed Mamma to eat some breakfast, I asked, experimentally: "Mamma, what would you say to going to an Oklahoma City hospital if I can get you in?" Her reply startled me, so sure was I of what she would say: "All right, if you'll go with me."

I could hardly believe my ears. Yet hope surged up in me and I heard myself saying recklessly, "Of course I'll go. The paper can manage without me if they have to."

Feeling committed now, certainty growing with each moment, I went back to the phone and called my brother in Oklahoma City, knowing he would just be getting home from the defense plant where he was a night foreman.

He was discouraging, too, at first. "I'll try, and I hope we can do it. But it's impossible to get anyone into a hospital without a doctor's commitment."

Of course I knew that, but I also knew something I couldn't tell him, or anyone. They might discredit that voice as being just a dream, but I couldn't. By then I was so sure about it that I had Mamma ready and her suitcase packed by the time his return call came.

"I haven't had any luck," he reported. "There's a vacancy coming up at noon in Wesley Hospital, but it's being held for a Dr. M——— there, who has a waiting list. There's nothing we can do now, but I'll keep trying and call you if anything comes up."

I might have given up then if I hadn't looked into the room where Mamma lay across her bed, dressed and quietly waiting. Wasn't that a miracle in itself? She must have heard, somewhere deep within herself, the same voice I'd heard. Why else had she changed so radically?

Then another thought came, like a flash of inspiration. Back I went to the phone, this time to call a dear friend who had been making frequent trips to the city to consult a doctor about her chronic heart condition. "Who is your Oklahoma City doctor?" I asked, and her reply almost took my breath away. He was Dr. M———, a member of the medical staff at Wesley, who had priority over the vacancy coming up. Even though my brother had been told that the physician had a waiting list of patients, I asked my friend if she would call him and see if he would accept my mother as a patient and get her admitted.

She was more than willing, and fifteen minutes later called to say the room was Mamma's if I could get her there by noon. None of his waiting paitents were critical, the doctor said, so if we considered Mamma to be, he would give her priority.

My hands were shaking as I thanked her and hung up, dazed at the way things were fitting into a pattern. Yet there were still hurdles. How could I get her there, and in a little over two hours? I'd have to have gas and my ration card wouldn't allow me enough without applying for emergency rations. That would take time. How could I make her comfortable for the long ride even if I had gas? And suppose that strange doctor wouldn't consider her condition critical after I got her there—if I could manage it.

While I pondered these questions, my brother called again to ask about Mamma and if there was anything more he could do. Yes, I heard myself saying, although the words seemed to come out without any willing them to on my part. "Call Dr. M——— and tell him I'll have Mamma there by noon." When I explained about my friend's call he was exuberant, but still worried. "Can you manage her alone?"

"I'll manage," I assured him. "Just meet us at the hospital and make sure the doctor is there."

Not until I actually committed myself did I have any idea how I'd make that sixty-mile drive in such a short time. But suddenly I felt I knew, and my next call was to the local undertaker, who had the only ambulance in town. If he had a funeral scheduled, that idea would not work out, but there were no doubts that God was managing everything, and perfectly. So I wasn't surprised to be assured that he'd get my mother there in time, and without any charge to me. He had not forgotten how many funerals my father had helped him with, never asking any pay.

Shortly after noon my poor mother was resting in the best hospital in the state, under the care of one of the best physicians, and I knew she was exactly where God wanted her to be. Even the nurse assigned to her care turned out to be an old school friend of Penny's with whom we'd lost contact after she moved away. She showered Mamma with loving care and attention. When Mamma died in that same hospital two months later, my heart was filled with gratitude to God for all the love with which he'd surrounded her during her last troubled days. Care and love she might have had sooner if, instead of giving reality to obstacles, I had released her to God's care. As much as he must have wanted to pour out his great love on her, I had blocked the way with my negativity, just as countless others stand in the way of letting divine love be manifested to and through them.

Not long ago I came across words in Paul's letter to the Philippians (4:12) that released this and a flood of other memories: "Everywhere and in all things I am instructed both to be full and to be hungry, both to abound and to suffer need."

Joy welled up in me, not because I had been "instructed" altogether with joyful experiences, but because each experience brought a joyful reality of the living presence of a Christ of love—counseling, loving, eternally providing, offering peace, just as Isaiah had prophesied he would.

Lovingly, wisely, Christ has taught me to say with the psalmist, "From the rising of the sun unto the going down thereof . . . . Our God shall come and shall not keep silence" (Ps. 50:1, 3).

9.

Supply for All Our Needs

AS IT WAS for most children, the Twenty-Third Psalm was the first Scripture I memorized. And, as it is for many adults, it is my favorite still. Yet it wasn't until I changed the words to read "I cannot want" that they became meaningful—warm and intimate and personal. For a quarter of a century the phrase has literally been my theme song, a constant reminder that I am not alone in fighting for survival in a world that at times seems cruelly indifferent.

God, Infinite Love, is never indifferent. There is no smallest need of mine that he is not acutely aware of, as though I am his only beloved child, as though the Shepherd had only one sheep. All I need do is trust his wisdom in determining those needs, as well as the manner in which they are met. And this, of course, is just the same for every living soul that recognizes it as truth.

Today we hear much about poverty and its effects upon the individual and upon society. The general assumption seems to be that poverty is synonymous with illiteracy and maladjustment. We automatically put the poor in worldly goods into the category of the underprivileged, when actually the opposite may be true. Poverty can also be a privilege if it contributes to a dependency upon, and a faith in, God which leads to a development of our own potential, as in the story of Job.

Without decrying any altruistic efforts to build a better America and a better world, some of us who were born into poverty or have lived with it without becoming defeated know that it cannot be eliminated from without, that it is a state of consciousness more than a condition. The recognition that within ourselves lives the limitless power of God makes each of us rich, no matter what has the appearance of lack.

This statement is supported by a classic Bible story in 2 Kings 4. Whether it is legendary or factual, that story has helped me through more than one acute crisis because I accept it as illustrating a literal truth. It is the story of a widow, so impoverished that the creditor of her deceased husband was threatening to make slaves of her two sons—a procedure legally acceptable then and for many centuries later.

This widow took her problem to the prophet Elisha, which in Israel was equivalent to turning to God, where such a prophet was looked upon as God's representative. Elisha did not offer her concrete help, for he was a poor man himself, as far as worldly goods went. Poor, but not needy. There is a vast difference, then and now. What he offered the poor widow was a challenge to help herself, outlining a project she would have rejected as an impossible assignment if she had not had implicit faith in God or in Elisha—or both. He told her to borrow all the vessels she could, then fill them with oil from the one small pot of oil that represented all her material possessions. Because she had the faith to comply, the impossible was accomplished. She was able to sell enough oil to pay her creditor and have security for herself and her sons from what was left.

With variations, I have had this same experience. It was mine when I took all the money I had and enrolled at the University of Oklahoma at the age of fifty-two to take special courses in professional writing in order to better equip myself to be independent, leaving my children free to live their own lives.

The challenge of faith was mine again when, after my mother's death, I moved to Oklahoma City to begin a career as a free-lance writer, with no other means of support. An impossibility, concerned friends and relatives warned me. A virtually inexperienced woman my age, no better equipped than I was, could not expect to support herself in such a highly competitive field. And this did not even take account of the fact that I had been in very poor health for several years.

It was not faith in myself per se that made me believe I could succeed, but faith in Christ's teaching that "with God" nothing is impossible. Having just read the late Glenn Clark's *The Soul's Sincere Desire,* I was ready to agree with him that any dream that possesses mind and heart to the exclusion of all other dreams is the voice of God—our destiny. Writing creatively instead of reportorially had become too compulsive a desire for me to ignore any longer.

So, at the age of fifty-five, with barely enough money to rent a small apartment and live for a month or so, if careful, and my only "pot of oil" a portable typewriter, I attempted the impossible. The fact that I did not know a single soul in the city, outside my brother's family, was all to the good, I thought. No interruptions. I was yet to learn that none of us can live on an island of self, wholly independent of his fellow-man. If we attempt to, we become independent of God, who lives within men, and thus become less than our highest selves.

Six years later, another compelling dream was born, another challenge to faith. At first I resisted the desire to write a religious novel, yielding only when it became so compulsive I could not concentrate upon the short stories and articles that had provided a somewhat insecure, but adequate, means of support. By then I had found a whole new world—dependable markets, friends, opportunities to help others. What more did I want?

Yet there was a deep need in me, the need that is every man's when he releases his life to God—the need to grow, to expand, to give of his best. Finally recognizing that I had reached another crossroad, I started in to fill large pots from my small one, a task that looked as impossible as did that of the widow who blazed a trail for us when she followed Elisha's counsel. Nothing is impossible where there is a strong enough faith.

For a few months all went well, although I soon found out that writing a book called for more concentration than anything I'd done before. To create characters that are flesh and blood people, not puppets or robots, one must imitate our Divine Creator and become one with his creation. As my work progressed, I ceased being a woman with a living to make, or one with social obligations, and became my main character—a woman in search of a faith to live by.

So it was like being jerked out of a dream world or off a rainbow to realize, when more than half through, that my small financial pot was completely empty. There was nothing out I had hopes of selling, no money left in the bank, and rent and utilities were past due. To be able to go on with the book meant I would have to lay it aside until I wrote and sold something else.

As though to remind me that the widow's oil did not stop flowing until she had no further needs to meet, in my mail that same day was a returned manuscript, accompanied by a request from an editor for a revision and cutting. Within two days that was accomplished, and with a song of praise to God I went back to the book. Yet I'd hardly become absorbed in it again when my mail brought warnings that my utilities would be cut off within a few days unless paid. Then the manager of the apartment house stopped by to remind me about the rent and to tell me something I hadn't yet found out—that my telephone had already been disconnected.

Even though I knew I could expect a fairly generous check in about a month, the fact did not solve my present embarrassing and acute situation. To make matters worse, my apartment building had recently changed hands and the new manager was also the owner. She was gracious and kind when I explained my failure to meet my obligations, but the worry in her eyes told me I had to redeem myself if we were to stay on friendly terms.

That night I took out neglected bills and added up the amount I had to have at once. I was dismayed to find the minimum to be one hundred and forty dollars, a comparatively small amount by today's standards. But it looked very big to a woman without any collateral to offer lending agencies, and who had made a vow to herself and her God that she would not burden her children, all of whom had problems of their own, in order to follow her own rainbow. Mike and I had been able to give them so little at a time of life when they needed so much in the way of security that I wanted more than anything to leave them free now to follow their own dreams—just as I was doing at last.

Was I going to have to abandon this particular dream? Even so, how could I find one hundred and forty dollars within forty-eight

hours? A little longer, for a glance at the calendar reminded me this
was Thursday. That meant a reprieve until Monday.

Picking up my Bible, I read again the story in Second Kings, finding myself murmuring aloud, childishly, as though a woman who may
never have lived at all could hear me. "Just what would you have
done if the oil had stopped flowing before your borrowed vessels
were half filled?"

Her reply came quickly, as clear and plain as though she stood
beside me in the flesh: *My oil couldn't stop. My faith wouldn't let it.*

Here was a challenge! Did I have that much faith? With all my
heart I wanted to, but deep inside me was a core of fear that kept
telling me I had to be practical and find a practical answer. Even
God couldn't help unless we helped ourselves. Or could he?

Almost feverishly I turned the pages of my Bible to read again
the psalm I'd found such comfort in before: "The Lord is my
shepherd; I shall not want. He maketh me to lie down in green
pastures: he leadeth me beside the still waters."

There was no need to read any further. Love and care throbbed
like a heartbeat in every word. I closed my eyes, mentally picturing
myself lying in a green meadow, in the midst of plenty; then I was
being lifted by a tender but firm hand and led beside a still lake, where
the sun danced on shimmering water like happy sprites at play. *Peace,*
a voice was whispering deep within me. *If I am your shepherd you
cannot want.*

Meaningful, comforting words. Relief was as strong as though
every want had already been supplied. After a restful night I went
back to work on the book, confident that my answer would come
before the weekend was over.

The manner in which it came still fills me with awe, eighteen
years and three books later. It may sound incredible to any reader
who has not experienced a miracle through stepping forth on God's
promises, but the woman he used to answer my need is still a close
friend and can attest to the truth of this story.

She had the face of a stranger, however, when I answered my
doorbell at dusk that Friday evening. Although we had met once at
the home of mutual friends, she had to remind me of that since we had
not exchanged more than a few words on that occasion. She lived in a

smaller town about twenty miles distant and explained that after completing an errand in our city she had yielded to a strong impulse to come by and get better acquainted. Would I go to dinner with her at a nearby cafeteria? Silently thanking God for sending me more than the cheese sandwich I'd planned to have, I accepted readily.

It was while we were eating that she suddenly asked, "Do you believe God answers prayers?"

"I surely do," I replied fervently. "If I didn't, I would not be enjoying this dinner and visiting with you as I am."

She smiled. "I thought you would say something like that. You know, I have a strong feeling God sent me to you for some special reason. Do you mind telling me what you've been praying about?"

Embarrassed, I explained that my problem was one of finances to be able to continue working on a book I was writing. It looked as though I might have to lay the project aside for a while, although I didn't feel that was what God wanted me to do.

"Then you won't have to," she said positively. "I think I know now what the Lord has been trying to tell me all day. I've a hundred dollars in the bank in what I call my emergency fund. If it will solve your problem, it's yours for as long as you need it."

How could I tell this generous stranger that I needed more than that? And how could I put myself under such obligation to a woman I'd just met? So I thanked her warmly, but declined, and considered the matter closed. Although I'd expressed faith in God, like many, many others who claimed to be believers, I was limiting his power to something less incredible than using strangers to help me. Yet when she left my apartment a couple of hours later her check lay on my table. How could I continue to refuse it? "You will make me disobey the Lord if you don't use this. I am convinced he sent me here tonight for this very purpose, as the urge was too strong to ignore," she had insisted earnestly.

For an instant I was tempted to tell her I needed forty dollars more, which was why I wasn't sure God had sent her to help me. After all, he knew how much I needed. Yet she was so eager to be his instrument of love that I resisted the impulse, laid the check in my Bible, and the next day all but forgot it as I continued work at my typewriter, still expecting a different answer.

That night she came back, just long enough to say she'd come across two bills tucked away in her Bible, money she'd meant to put into the "emergency" fund, but had neglected to take care of. Again she'd yielded to the urge to bring them to me, afraid the hundred dollars might not be enough. Even before I looked at them I'd known the size of those bills. Both were twenties, adding up to the exact amount I had to have right away. Yet this woman could not have known that, for no amount had ever been mentioned between us. Only God knew.

A few weeks later the manuscript was in the hands of a literary agent, and I felt no concern about it as I started building up a back-log of shorter pieces. Since God had brought me this far, he would take me the rest of the way.

One morning during my meditation period, while I was reading in Hebrews, one sentence seemed suddenly to separate itself from the rest of the text, standing out alone in stark boldness, yet having no special significance in itself. It was the rush of joyful response in me that gave the words significance. Reading again and again the simple message, "I have written a letter unto you in a few words" (Heb. 13:22), I knew beyond all doubt that they contained a meaningful message especially for me. And I was sure what that message was.

Going to the telephone, I called my new friend God had sent me. "My book has sold," I told her. After she expressed her joy, she asked the natural question, "Who to?"

"I don't know," I admitted, "but I'm sure it has."

After I told her of my cryptic "message" she agreed with me enthusiastically. "I'll drive in tonight and we'll go to dinner to celebrate," she added.

It was a joyous, though quiet, celebration, with both of us expressing praise and thanksgiving to God, not even wondering who my publisher would be. It was enough for both of us that God was directing things. And neither of us was surprised when we returned to my apartment to find the telegram from my new agent lying under my door. A letter from God in a few words!

This is only one of many instances when my material needs were met in miraculous ways after I learned to release all my affairs to God, to let him become my business agent as truly as though he had the form of man. That does not mean that all my wants were met, of course. Our God is wise beyond human ability to separate desires from needs.

There was, as another instance of God's willingness to supply our needs, what I recall happily as my "raven Christmas." A long illness, following major surgery, had reduced me to a state very close to acute need; yet I knew I had no reason to fear. As soon as I was able to return to work, everything would be all right. In the meantime I could trust in God, just as Elijah had when he was fed by ravens.

When Christmas cards started coming from friends and relatives in distant states, it was almost amazing to find that practically every one contained a small bill or check, although I had not broadcast my situation. When I totalled them all up, the amount came to one hundred and eighty dollars—almost the exact amount I owed my patient physician and all voluntary gifts of love from unexpected sources. And why not? God's "habitation" is in human hearts and he speaks with "a mighty voice" to inspire deeds of love, sometimes without the conscious awareness of the one to whom he speaks.

Yet, God has also taught me, he never takes from one to give to another without rewarding the giver as well as the receiver. That is an inflexible spiritual law. Whatever we sow, we reap. Whatever we give in his name—in love—is rewarded, even if the gift is no more than a cup of cold water to a thirsty traveler, a kind word of comfort or encouragement, or a sharing of our material things. All have the same evaluation in the eyes of God.

That knowledge is one of many reasons why my heart has learned to sing with the psalmist, "Great is our Lord, and of great power: his understanding is infinite" (147:5).

Infinite understanding of our needs, infinite love in supplying all those needs is ours when we give him total trust. And that trust makes the poor rich, whatever their degree of supply appears to be—rich in security and peace.

10.

The Healing Touch

WE HAVE SAID the Bible is a bridge across time, spanning the centuries, fusing today into yesterday and yesterday into today. On a night in 1948 I crossed that bridge and became the woman of Capernaum who received healing by barely touching the garments of Jesus. Healing through the touch of faith.

Often the question arises Do you believe in faith healings? The only answer to that is a counterquestion: Do you believe in God? Jesus said of the miraculous healings he was able to do that "the Father that dwelleth in me, he doeth the works" (John 14:10). Has God changed with time?

Healing of the sick was an important part of the ministry of Jesus. He came into a world of sick bodies and sick minds, different from our world of today only in that such suffering was accepted as a way of life. Agencies of healing such as those available to the masses today were unknown then, and Jesus brought hope into a hopeless world by his great compassion for the sick, the lame, and the blind. If we judge by the records left by the apostolic writers, he gave as much attention to sick bodies as to sick souls, which seems to indicate that he saw no separation of soul from body—only the difference that one outlives the other.

Yet with all his compassion, Jesus could not have healed all the sick he saw. We have records of where he succeeded, but not of the instances where he failed because of lack of faith on the part of the suffering one. So the question of whether healing through faith today is possible has to be answered with reservations, just as

Jesus himself often answered a plea for help by asking, "Dost thou believe?"

Any healing today, as then, depends upon the degree of faith the sufferer has in the treatment offered him. Any physician will admit that he can only offer the knowledge of miracle drugs, surgical techniques, and therapeutic treatments. Acceptance of them through faith is up to the patient. Sometimes this is called "the will to live," but desire can be defeated through lack of faith in the help offered.

Faith, Paul says, is the substance of things desired, or hoped for. Substance is material matter. Reality. Any complete acceptance of good to replace ill, by whatever process, that inspires faith in the patient can be called faith healing. To arbitrarily demand that such healings must come about through certain methods prescribed by men indicates a faith which limits God's power in its seeking to work through men. Just as limiting, however, can be the arbitrary demand that healing must be brought about without such human aids.

This refusal to use human aid is the method usually categorized as faith healing, but more often than not human aid is involved in those cases also. Whatever prayers are said over or for those in need of healing, whatever "laying on of hands" or other dramatic actions are performed, are human aids given to strengthen the patient's faith.

Nor can such aids to faith be classified per se as deception. Jesus himself often resorted to them. He used clay made of spittle and the dust of the road to heal a blind man whose weak faith demanded evidence that Jesus had supernatural powers; he laid his hands over the eyes of another, wanting him to feel the love vibrating through them and believe; to another he spoke only the loving words, "Receive thy sight." The results in each case were the same. His methods must have differed only because in each case the degree of faith offered him differed.

Truth is eternal, not changing with time. Healings today, like healings Jesus brought about and those performed by men in whom the sick had faith centuries before he walked the earth, are possible only through methods the mind, body, and soul can accept in harmonious unity. You may find healing in a modern hospital, with all its facilities for strengthening faith; or in the church as you kneel at an altar with another imploring God's mercy for you, if your faith demands intercessory prayer; or in the solitude of a desert place, with no human help available; or in the stillness of your own soul when fear is routed through secret prayer. The method is not as important as the faith you have in that method. "Dost thou believe?"

Only belief in a divine power that transcends our limited humanity can contribute to this inner harmony we call faith. Without it there can be no healing of mind, body, and soul. With it all things are possible. We have only to reach out in joyful expectation, as did the woman in Capernaum, and contact divine love, given reality through faith. She had, according to the story told by Luke (ch. 8) suffered for twelve years and "spent all her living upon physicians, neither could be healed of any"; yet was healed instantly through barely touching the robe of Jesus.

To what did Jesus himself credit that healing? Not to his love, as great as it was for all sufferers; not even to her belief in God, although without that belief she would never have gone looking for the man she must have believed came from God; and certainly he did not claim there was healing power in his clothing. "Thy faith hath made thee whole," he told her—the unqualified faith that inspired her reaching.

How grateful I am to this nameless woman that she transmitted her faith to me the night I lay in a Dallas hospital, facing the same experience as had been hers. Not afraid of dying, but terribly, terribly afraid of living with the inoperable malignancy an Oklahoma City gynecologist was convinced I had but said he could not be certain about without a biopsy. My son's plea to be with me when my fate was determined had made me enter a Dallas hospital, under the care of a physician recommended by friends of his.

This physician disagreed with the diagnosis previously given me. So sure was he that there was no malignancy that he left me on the operating table after the biopsy while the laboratory test was being made. Forty minutes later he came back to announce triumphantly that the test had proved negative, just as he'd expected. Then he used an electric needle to give me a complete curettage. That night my son and his family danced a jig around my bed to show their happiness, and the next day I was allowed to go to their home for a short recuperation before returning to Oklahoma.

The severe pains began about dusk but I endured them, assuming they were a natural result of the curettage. By midnight I began running a high temperature, accompanied by violent chills and increasing pain. My son's efforts to locate my doctor proved fruitless as he'd left the city for the weekend without saying where he could be reached. By morning I was in agony, and my son called the hospital, asking to have me readmitted. Their reply to his request was to send an ambulance, siren screaming. A mistake had been made in the laboratory, due to an unusual coincidence of similar names. My report should have read positive instead of negative.

At the hospital a radiologist was waiting for me, with nurses standing by, and I did not need to be told that my condition was serious. With cancer cells scattered by that well-meant treatment given me, infection had set in.

It was night again when I came out of the anesthetic and back into excruciating pain, finding myself packed with radium needles and forced to lie rigidly still on a hard, pillowless bed. The pain in my body, as severe as it was, was more endurable than the tormenting pain that knowledge of my condition brought. What did it matter if I did recover from the infection, only to face a more lingering death from cancer, a terrible burden on the children I loved and had wanted to leave free?

Only too well I knew that cancer of the cervix (at that time) was rated as one of the most deadly forms of malignancy but the slowest to kill. A close friend had lingered for six years with the condition, and I had seen the toll exacted from her family. How could I bear doing that to mine?

Although I tried to pray, my feverish lips whispered only disconnected words. Lost in the confusion of fear and pain, God seemed very far away. Pain was closer, fear and despair stronger.

It must have been near midnight when the nurse gave me more sedation, then tiptoed from the room, thinking I slept. She was wrong, for I was fully conscious of the sounds and atmosphere of the hospital and of the intense pain in my body. I felt as though mind and body were being pressed in a vise from which there was no hope of freeing myself.

Then suddenly I was recalling the biblical story of the woman who must have suffered from the same condition I had to accept, and it was as though she materialized out of the dim past and stood beside my bed, reminding me of how she had been set free from the vise in which I felt caught. Bits of the story began floating through my feverish mind, and I fastened my thoughts upon them, trying to fit the pieces together. Great envy for that other woman filled me. At least she had been free enough to go looking for Jesus, but I had to lie rigid on this bed, unmoving, helpless.

Yet it seemed to me she was beckoning me to follow her, and suddenly I no longer lay on that hospital bed. Instead I, too, had gone in search of the Healer of Nazareth. I must be that other woman, I thought, for I could see the sun shimmering on the waters of Lake Galilee, smell the tangy odor of fish in the marketplaces as I wandered about, whispering the words she had used: "If I can but touch him . . . "

When I felt myself a part of a jostling crowd I knew Jesus was near. Faces and bodies pressed against me, smotheringly close, but I kept pushing and reaching, pleading to be allowed to get through so I could touch him and be healed.

Something happened then which I make no attempt to rationalize. The crowd disappeared and again I was alone, but still reaching, reaching, to contact the Healer I could not see but knew was there. And close. Suddenly a soft glow seemed to fill the dim room and Something came toward my bed. Not a form or face, just a moving glow, softly lustrous, faintly iridescent. My heart leaped, my whole body tingled as though an electric current had passed through it. Perhaps I cried out, for the door opened and the nurse hurried in, asking if I had called.

The glow vanished when she entered, but not the wonder and awe, the joy pulsing through me. These stayed with me. After the nurse had left again, I discovered the pain had vanished and with it all my fears. I had touched the Christ. Just a bare touch, but it was enough. There was no doubt in my heart then, or since, that my healing had taken place.

My recovery was rapid. For the peace of mind of my family, none of whom had shared my sacred moment of healing, I submitted to ninety–six hours of radium treatment and all the powerful x-ray therapy they dared use. Yet a month later I was back at my desk in my own home, with no apparent ill effects.

A test of my faith came shortly after I returned home. A nationally known exponent of faith healings, the late Dr. Rebecca Beard, author and physician, came to Oklahoma City, and concerned friends invited me to hear her. During the healing session that followed her lecture they urged me to join those asking for her prayers. They were unable to understand my refusal. "Even if you do feel you've been healed," they argued, "prayer won't hurt you."

They were wrong, as Doctor Beard herself agreed when I explained my refusal to her. To have accepted further petitioning to God for what I knew I'd already been given might have opened doors to doubt in the days or years ahead. Once my mind entertained any thought of further need, my faith might have started to waver, opening doors to fears, and my healing could have been lost. As it is, I am as sure today as I was twenty-one years ago that my healing came in the same manner as it had to that woman who saw Jesus in the flesh.

When the Dallas radiologist gave me my final five-year checkup, he admitted, "Yours has been a remarkable recovery. Five years ago I didn't give you much chance."

I didn't tell that conscientious man of science, who had used all his technical training to help me, that I gave God rather than him the credit for my healing. That would not have been literally true, for I believe—know—that God uses dedicated men of science as his instruments of love; that all modern medical discoveries and advanced techniques are gifts from him.

Yet I also know that God's is the power, with or without these aids to faith. His is the love that activates the healing power, expressing itself to us in whatever way our minds will accept.

Nothing can happen to our bodies without the conscious or unconscious consent of the mind, psychologists tell us, but the mind can betray us as truly as Judas betrayed Jesus.

Only faith can save and heal—faith in a living God of love.

11.

He Will Direct Thy Paths

A NUMBER of years ago I heard a radio minister whose name I have forgotten use an illustration I shall never forget. Too many of us, he said, prayed in order to tell God what he should do instead of asking him what we should do. "We put ourselves in the harness to pull the cart, expecting God to stay behind and push," he declared.

This is a graphic, if slightly crude, analogy. Too often we do take our problems to God, asking only that we be given what we feel we should have, not what his wisdom dictates. We do not want to be led, only helped, an attitude from which has risen a faith philosophy that we can have anything we want by turning to God in prayer.

This could not be what Jesus was teaching when he said, "Ask and you shall receive," nor when he told his disciples that if they had faith "as a grain of mustard seed" they could remove mountains. Often this phrase is made to read as though Jesus were comparing the size of the disciples' faith with a tiny seed, as does the New English Bible and also the Moffatt translation. The King James use of the word *as,* or *like,* indicates a deeper, more meaningful truth. It speaks of a living faith and of trust in the limitless love of God. A seed does not ask how or to what size it shall grow. It just grows according to the life force given it of God. To have faith like that seed we do not limit God's power, as those disciples were doing the day they failed to heal an epileptic boy (Matt. 17). Neither do we attempt to dictate to God the manner in which we grow and develop and bear fruit for him. Instead we say with Jesus, "Not my will but thine be done." We give him trust as well as faith.

Unless taken out of context, there is no promise that God grants every desire we take to him. We do not have that permissive a heavenly father, and I am glad, for my human wisdom falls far short of knowing what is best for me or for others for whom I pray. Yet instead of letting him dictate and supply my needs, the temptation is always there to list my wants for him—a human weakness that accounts for every lack in my life, every failure I've made to demonstrate the power of God's unfailing love. And the same is true of everyone. Until we release our ideas and our desires to him, there cannot be a free-flowing of his love, perfect expression of his good.

This truth is emphasized in one of the most inspirational of the maxims we know as the Proverbs, presumed to have been written by the very wise King Solomon: "Trust in the Lord with all thine heart; and lean not unto thine own understanding. In all thy ways acknowledge him, and he shall direct thy paths" (3:5–6).

What more can we ask than that our paths in life be directed by a God of love? Then every day becomes an adventure in living, peace and security ours under all circumstances. Yet this, like all the goals we would aspire to, is dependent upon meeting certain conditions. According to this writer, there are three to be met before God will take over our lives, directing us in ways that lead to spiritual maturity. First, we must give him implicit trust, total acceptance of him as Ruler; second, we must release all ideas and all desires of our own; third, we must not withhold any area of our life, recognizing that he is concerned with every smallest detail of that which affects us.

Until we meet these conditions there cannot be the rapport that gives God reality, the authority he must have before assuming the position of Ruler, King, Counselor, Friend—all the things Isaiah says he stands ready to be to us through the coming into the world of a Savior who takes the government, the directing of our paths, upon his shoulder (Isa. 9:6). Until we put the governing power in his hands in complete trust, he can only wait, as did the loving parent in the parable of the prodigal son, until we see the error of our ways, the futility of wandering about in want, and return "home." Then how we welcome God's wisdom, how joyfully we feast instead of starving, how trustingly we put our hand in his to be led.

How exciting, but how peaceful, life can be with God directing us in small things as well as large. Yet can we consider any experience small that keeps us aware of the indwelling Holy Spirit? All our ways, the important and the seemingly unimportant, are the same in the eyes of God—our thoughts, our attitudes, our actions. There is nothing that affects our character, our personality, or our spiritual growth about which he is not concerned.

How can we be sure we are being led by him and not by our own human desires? This was a question often raised in my Bible study group, and there seems only one answer. When we follow the dictates of love, we are being led by God who is love, and there is peace and joy in our hearts. When we make mistakes and take the wrong paths, our hearts will know, for the peace and joy will be lost. Even then, however, our all-wise and all-loving heavenly father stands ready to rectify our mistakes and bring us back out of chaos into the shelter of his wisdom and love.

To insure this God-guidance we need only to establish rapport and thus his reality. Then communication is established, through which we are made aware of the path we should take.

There are many ways of communicating with the indwelling Christ-Spirit, but there is only one designed for each of us. Our heart's response will tell us when we have found that way. It may be through prayer, after we have mastered the art of stilling our minds and listening for the divine voice. There is no true communication without this stillness on our part. Petitioning prayer may block the stream of conscious awareness through giving more reality to our needs than to God's love.

Of course any form of communication with God is prayer, although prayer, as it is often defined, may fail completely to be communication when it takes the form of words spoken only as a ritual. If communication is established through rapport, the manner in which prayer is made is not important. My father and his contemporaries believed that prayer called for certain postures, usually the one of getting down upon their knees. Today's religious leaders recognize that more often than not the petitioner forced to assume such a position is too uncomfortable physically to become wholly engrossed spiritually. A relaxed position is more generally advocated, but there may be times and circumstances when we feel closer to God through the sacrifice of comfort and the sense of humility indicated by praying upon our knees.

Many spiritually developed souls do not need any certain form or system of communication to hear and recognize the "still small voice." The stranger who appeared at my door to answer my prayer for financial help had been sitting in a dentist's chair undergoing the ordeal of having a tooth filled when she heard God's voice directing her to go to me. She could easily have dismissed the impulse under the circumstances, but love had taught her how to distinguish the voice of him who is love. The heart living in attunement with God will recognize his voice.

Living in attunement is what Paul must have been referring to when he wrote to the Thessalonians to "pray without ceasing" (1 Thess. 5:17). He would have been asking the impossible of humans if he had not been referring to an attitude of mind rather than a ritual. This is the attitude that should be the goal of every Christian, the purpose in finding one's own method of communication.

The Bible, which a Christian world recognizes as "the word of God" and which Word the psalmist calls a lamp for our feet, can provide communication leading to this desired state of attunement when we approach it lovingly and prayerfully. Since childhood, love for the Scriptures has given the Bible a voice for me, often strengthening my faith when it faltered. It is always a reminder of God's unfailing love, and a source of joy and praise that establishes rapport whatever my mental state, so long as I keep the candle of faith burning.

"Rejoice evermore," Paul also enjoined the Thessalonians, another human impossibility without complete trust that God is leading us along the paths he wants us to travel. Jesus phrased this same thought in the form of a warning when he told his ambitious disciples, "Except ye be converted [change your attitude], and become as little children, ye shall not enter into the kingdom of heaven" (Matt. 18:3).

Since he also taught that the kingdom is within the human heart, or consciousness, he had to be warning them they could not be led by their indwelling God-Spirit until they released their own selfish goals, their limiting ideas. A small child does not argue and reason when a trusted parent takes his hand to lead him through the darkness of night. Trust makes the child feel safe, even though he cannot see the way he is being led, or why.

To acquire this childish trust in God's guidance is to live in the kingdom, here and now, but without any diminishing of. mental powers or loss of self-identity. On the contrary, only as we learn to live in continual Spirit-guidance can we come into fulfillment of those mental powers and into knowledge of true self-identity, into a rewarding and meaningful life.

Such a life may not appear rewarding to those who judge by worldly standards or who prefer to direct their own paths. But the heart that knows total reliance upon God experiences a peace and joy not found in outer conditions, regardless of the paths he directs us to take. One of the most joyous personalities I ever knew was a young woman so crippled with arthritis that she had no use of her twisted feet and little use of her misshapen hands. Yet she lived in the kingdom, literally obeying Paul's injunction to "rejoice evermore," even in hours of pain that would have defeated one without her unfaltering faith in God's love. Because she knew what rapport with him can mean to enhance the joy of living, she strapped a pencil to her pain-twisted finger and typed out messages of praise to share with others.

Another joyous Christian I know is a woman bedfast with multiple sclerosis. Though her path has led her in and out of hospitals for many years, that fact has not dimmed her joy in a God-relationship that gives life a meaning it would not have otherwise. It is impossible to evaluate the contribution she has made to others by inspiring faith in them through the quiet confidence of her own faith.

These two and countless others like them—those bearing burdens of illness and other physical handicaps, burdens of age that virtually isolate them from the world, and burdens of poverty that are no fault of their own—all make up an influential underground church in the Christian world that gets little or no recognition from ecclesiastical leaders because its members blow no trumpets. They are faceless and nameless. Yet, though their audiences also are faceless, their songs of praise and triumph are heard throughout the world. Without podiums to preach from, without organizational powers, without trumpets to call attention to their good deeds, they are living refutation of the teaching being advanced by some modern theologians that the need of a personal Savior is outdated. Without a personal God-relationship, how could these anonymous saints keep a song in their hearts while traveling the rough paths of their destinies?

While I recognize that the ones decrying the need of a personal Savior are referring to the ultimate salvation of the soul, my Bible makes it plain to me that whatever we are in this life will affect what we are in the next. We are not measured by the quantity of good deeds the world may or may not notice, but by the quality of faith and love in our hearts. Without a personal Savior, a Spirit-guide to keep our feet on the right path, what wasted lives most of us would lead! And if today is wasted, there will be also a wasted tomorrow.

For many years, dating from my teens, I gave a zealous loyalty to my church and all its activities but knew little about the rapport found only in meditating in solitude. Nor did I know the happiness to be found in serving for the pure joy of sharing truth and praise and love until I turned from outer things into the inner place of God's habitation. Then I no longer wanted to dictate the ways in which I should serve him nor the manner in which I served others. After having asked him to direct my path, to become my personal Savior in achieving spiritual maturity, I had to be willing to go the way he directed. And his hand led me into experiences of joy and into quiet pools of peace such as I had never known before.

As an illustration: As an active church worker I had found much pleasure in speaking to women's and youth organizations and once had literally preached to a gathering of three hundred ministers. Happy as many of these occasions were, none gave me the deep inner joy that was mine in recent years from talking to an audience of one, an experience I shall never forget.

It happened the day of a monthly luncheon meeting of a writers' organization to which I belonged. I'd been looking forward to the meeting and to giving the short talk the program chairman had asked me to make. Just as I was about to leave my apartment, however, my doorbell rang. When I answered it, I found a man standing there whom I had not seen in almost a year. Once he and I had belonged to the same prayer group, but he had dropped out after his young wife divorced him to marry another man. Before his marriage to her he had been a heavy drinker, and we'd heard that he'd gone back to drinking again.

Surprised to find him at my door and a little perturbed to see plainly that he'd been drinking, my first reaction was one of dismay that I might be delayed, as I barely had time to make my luncheon. He noticed my hesitation and asked, "Are you going somewhere?"

I started to say yes and suggest that he come another time when something stopped me—perhaps his bloodshot eyes and haggard face; perhaps the thought, so strong it was like a voice inside me, *he needs to talk to someone*. So I opened the door wider and invited him in, saying I was in no hurry.

He came in but stood looking at me from unhappy, brooding eyes. "I've no business barging in on you like this. I was just driving by and—well, I just felt like maybe I could talk to you."

By then I was so conscious of some deep need in him that I forgot the meeting I'd anticipated. (That is the way God works his will in us.) "Sit down, Bill, and relax," I said. (Bill wasn't his name but it will do.) "I'll get us some coffee and then we'll talk."

Two hours later we were still talking. At first I'd only listened while Bill poured out his inner conflicts like water bursting over a dam. Listening, I could sense the deep well of loneliness inside him, the guilt that made him feel isolated from all he'd wanted to do with his life. "I know I'm a real backslider," he said miserably. "I just couldn't take what was handed out to me."

"If you'd kept coming to the meetings, we might have been able to help you," I reminded him gently.

"Are you kidding?" he said gruffly. "Who'd want a lush like me around? Everybody knows I've been hitting the bottle pretty hard since Sylvia walked out on me."

"Why, Bill?" I asked. "That doesn't solve anything."

He shrugged. "Maybe just a sort of tranquilizer. But you wouldn't understand about that."

"Perhaps I do," I told him. "And what's more important, God understands."

He looked a little incredulous. "You mean he hasn't washed his hands of me?"

That was the opening I needed, so I began to talk about the great love of God, how willingly he forgives our mistakes, how he gives us strength to overcome our weaknesses when we ask him to, how his love can heal the hurts others give us. I reminded him of the parable of the prodigal son—how joyfully the son was received when he "came to himself" ("got wise" in today's venacular) and realized it was by his own choice that he ate with swine instead of enjoying a good life in his father's house.

Bill, relaxed now, laughed at my comparison. "That's me, all right, lining up with the swine." Then he became serious, and there was a pleading, childishly wistful note in his voice as he asked, "Do you really think God would take me back if I asked him?"

It was my turn to smile. "You don't even have to ask, my friend. The prodigal didn't. Remember? He just decided to go back, and his father was so glad to see him that he didn't even listen to his speech of repentance."

Bill said thoughtfully, "That's an idea. I guess he knows all the things I'd like to say if I knew how."

When he finally stood up to leave he seemed to stand taller, a new light in his eyes. "I think the Big Boss sent me here to get you to stiffen my backbone," he said in his man-talk style. "Tell him I said thanks, will you? It sure helps to feel there's Somebody on my team batting for me. Maybe I'll start back to the meetings when I dry out."

Yes, there had been Somebody on Bill's team. That was my first thought when I read in the next morning's paper that Bill had been killed in an accident in the shop where he worked as a mechanic. A jack had slipped, crushing him under a car. Recalling the new light in his face when he'd left me a few hours earlier, I whispered a fervent, "Thank you, Father. Thanks from Bill and from me."

That God, Holy Spirit of Love, had sent Bill to me I had no doubt. How glad I was that I had not turned him away as was my first impulse. Although I'd had no intuition that he was being prepared to make his transition, God had known and wanted Bill to be reminded of the love that would take him "over his Jordan" and into the land (or consciousness) of beginning again.

That is the greatness of our God, Love Incarnate. No one lives outside that love unless he chooses to. And living in it is like living in an impregnable fort, securely protected from enemies attacking from without or within. It is the happy state Paul referred to when he wrote, "For me to live is Christ." Not comparing our weak humanity with his perfection, but letting that perfection guide us as he longs to do. Not only leading us into ways of service, but also into ways of pleasure when we are willing trustingly to follow his direction.

Such adventures in faith may often violate our human desires or logical instincts. Though this has often happened to me, I can truthfully say that never have I regretted obeying the voice my heart told me was God's instead of letting reason dictate. Only God can number the times I missed happy experiences through failure to hear or to trust that guidance.

A small incident comes to mind. I was visiting in the home of my son in Houston, Texas, when I had a sudden urge to leave two days earlier than I'd planned. My son was puzzled. "Why this sudden rush, Mother? I don't get it."

"Neither do I," I admitted, because he is very understanding. "I just know there is some reason why I should take this particular train."

The reason became apparent to both of us as we entered the coach the next morning. Someone called my name from the other end of the car, and seconds later I was embracing a dear friend I had not seen for several years. Our destination was the same, and we had a full day's happy visiting together. Love-power at work—had I resisted its guidance I would have missed that day's pleasure without ever being aware of what might have been.

A great many marvelous experiences have happened to me as a result of letting God become the authority in my life. More could be told if space permitted, although some are almost too personal, or too traumatic, to be credible. All demonstrate the truth that we do not walk alone, that God is as interested in the routine affairs of daily living as in the more spectacular; that he goes ahead of each of us, where there is love and trust, to make smooth the way.

Isaiah sums it up well: "And a highway shall be there . . . wayfaring men, though fools, shall not err therein" (35:8). Shall not err when we are attuned to his wisdom and his love.

12.

Light in the Dark of Night

RECENTLY during a visit in the home of my son, one morning while I was having my quiet time of meditation, as is my custom, my grandson came into the room. Seeing the Bible in my lap, his eyes lit up with interest, and he came over to squat beside my chair. "What did God say to you this morning, Grandma?" he asked.

For a moment the lump in my throat made it hard to answer. Then I lightly touched his dark wavy hair, smiled into his intent dark eyes and said gently, "He spoke of his love for us and said he will take care of us if we trust him."

The light in his eyes became a glow. "Even when I have to go back to the hospital?"

"Especially then, darling. We just have to know he helps us whenever we need him most. And he always knows what's best for us."

He relaxed visibly, then fairly startled me by saying, "We just let the government be on his shoulders, eh?"

Startling words to come from the lips of a youth who had never been able to read the Bible, to attend Sunday school or church services, and who had spent the past ten years in an institution for the mentally ill. No, hardly a youth, for chronologically he was twenty-eight years old; yet not a man, for mentally he was not yet in his teens.

When had he heard and memorized Isaiah's prophecy? From his parents or myself? From another hospital inmate or a nurse?

Perhaps any of these. Yet I had the distinct feeling that he was hearing them for the first time as he spoke them; that the God we were talking about was saying them to and through him, offering him reassurance because of the unnamed fears he constantly battled, the dread of returning to the institution that was always his during the infrequent visits he was allowed to make to the home from which he'd been exiled through no fault of his.

Our God is like that. Although invisible, he is not unreal or lacking in power, and surely never lacking in love and understanding. How well I know that from my own experience, and from the experience of those who walked our paths ahead of us—those whose stories have been preserved as a light for us who follow them.

Long after my grandson had gone back to his room to enjoy the toys that always waited for him as did the little tin soldier of a song I used to sing to my children, I sat there pouring out thanks to God for having given us this boy to love and to be loved by. Only God could know how much that love had enriched our lives, for the world gave us only pity—the degrading pity so often offered the handicapped.

The house was very quiet, both my son and his wife having left for their respective jobs; yet it wasn't empty, for it seemed as though two other parents had crossed centuries of time and sat there with me. They reminded me, as both had many times before, that it is when we reach the limit of our human ability to help our loved ones that God takes over. Now they sat with me in an hour of thanksgiving, but both had shared many black hours with me, when there was only grief and despair in my heart. They had had to remind me more than once that God never forsakes us when we fully trust him.

The younger of the two fathers lived in the time of Jesus, the other many centuries before that; both had exhibited the faith that works miracles, a light for all troubled parents of today. Although their problems were not alike, their emotional experiences were: both saw the blackness of night, and both, through turning to God in love and trust, saw light. One brought his afflicted son and laid him at the feet of Jesus; the parent from earlier times laid his beloved son upon an altar as evidence of his total trust in God's wisdom and love.

In the New Testament story the father evidenced a great faith in Jesus by asking healing for his son, an epileptic. At that time, and for centuries after, the disease was considered hopeless. Even worse, the sufferer was presumed to be possessed by evil spirits, which made him an object of scorn rather than pity. But this parent loved his son enough to seek out the Healer of Galilee to ask help for him.

Even as he asked for that help, his son suffered an attack and fell to the ground, writhing in torment and foaming at the mouth. The crowd that had gathered to watch must have moved back in horror then, but there could have been only compassion in Jesus' voice as he asked how long the youth had been afflicted.

"Since he was a child," we hear the father reply. Then he added his prayer that expressed a little less than total faith: "If thou canst do anything, have compassion on us and help us."

How often we pray prayers like that today, prayers with *ifs* that limit God's power. So the reply of Jesus was said to all the living now as well as then: "All things are possible to him that believeth." Then the agonized parent laid all his burdens upon Jesus as he said, "Lord, I believe; help thou mine unbelief." And Jesus understood this prayer that referred to the enormity of the man's burden, so great that it was almost beyond human ability to believe it could be lifted. A few minutes later the man left the scene, happy and relieved because, as Matthew reports, "the child was healed from that very hour."

In the beginning of our long night I prayed this father's prayer over and over. Even though I had sound reason to believe in faith healings, the core of doubt, the *if*, lay deep in my heart. Our boy had suffered a brain damage at birth, when he was stillborn and seemingly dead for forty-five minutes. Through the efforts of the small town physician he was revived, but enough of his brain was damaged that he lacked balance and coordination of thought processes. That God could heal, I had no doubts. But could he restore that vital part that had been destroyed? Had I a right to ask it? Had I the human ability to wholly accept it?

Deep in my heart there were reservations I could not lose as the years passed and the boy's retardation became more and more apparent, in spite of his father's refusal to admit it. The child was lovable and docile and unusually beautiful, and soon became the center of our world. After it was determined that he could not endure the pressures of competition in the public school, his parents and two older sisters made every sacrifice to obtain the best medical and psychiatric help possible and to send him to the most expensive private schools.

In spite of the heavy financial burden on his parents, the early years were not unrewarding, for love is never that. Even after the schools had to be marked off as failures, my son, unable to abandon hope for his only son, in the boy's teen years put him in the hands of a private tutor who was highly optimistic that he could help him achieve normalcy. The problem was mainly one of personality, he declared. The boy only needed to be released from emotional inhibitions, aroused to throw off repressions and accept himself as being capable of self-expression.

This experiment of playing God proved disastrous. Within a year or so we saw our confused but gentle boy turning into an erratic youth tormented by aroused emotions he could not understand, driven by dark impulses beyond his power to control, bitterly resentful that he could not enjoy the privileges he saw other boys his age enjoying, terrified at the awareness that he was a misfit in a world he longed to be a part of. As his tendency toward violent rebellion increased, our loving concern for him changed to acute fear and our real Gethsemane began.

"Promise me you'll never institutionalize him," I unwisely begged my son during a visit in his home. "I couldn't bear to see that happen to him." And, as we are all prone to do, I tried to tell God what was best for the boy. "Don't let that happen to him," I prayed, over and over.

So I thought my heart would break the night my son telephoned long distance to say it had happened. Our boy's confused mind had cracked under the strain of trying to adjust to a world that terrified him and he'd had to be forcibly restrained and locked away.

"Mother, we had to do it," my son said, brokenly. "He tried to hurt himself and his mother. This wasn't the first time but I couldn't bear to tell you sooner."

In the double agony of suffering for my loved ones and for the boy I loved as my own, I felt for a while that all my prayers and my faith had been futile. I was lying across my bed, giving way to wild grief and bitter tears when my phone rang again, so insistently that I forced myself to answer. A friend's agitated voice asked if I had my television turned on. When I said no, she demanded excitedly, "Turn it on quick."

Leaving the phone, I hurried to do as she had asked and found myself listening in horror to the account of the brutal murder of another friend and her husband at the hands of their only son, a youth she had admitted to me only a few weeks before she was worried about because he had grown so antagonistic toward his parents.

After I'd recovered from the shock of the news, I went back to my bed, but not to give way to tears again. This time I fell on my knees and poured out my thanks to God that the boy I loved was where he was, protected from harming himself or others; spared the tragedy that other youth must live with forever. And I prayed for that boy and for all the confused youth in our confusing world.

So, together with my son and his gentle wife I came to understand how an aged father named Abraham could hold a knife over his beloved son after he'd laid him on the altar. Love gives us strength to do what has to be done for our loved ones. Like that aged father in time, we had to release ours to God, then see him strapped to his bed like a wild animal and walk away from the torture chamber with dry eyes and uplifted head, in essence saying to the world what Abraham said to his servants before starting up the mountain to sacrifice his Isaac: "Sit ye here . . . we will go and worship and come again to you."

Now, ten years later and with our loved one still shut away from the world most of the time, I can truthfully say the experience has been one of worship. Trust in Him is the worship God asks, and this trust has grown for all of us as we've watched our handicapped youth's brave fight to control his inner conflicts and observed the advanced methods of helping such sick, confused minds.

From my sideline position I have seen my son acquire a spiritual stature that fills my heart with thanksgiving and makes me "lift up my eyes" above the devastating financial burden he is still carrying, the sacrifices he has been compelled to make; I have watched his lovely wife, as dear to me as my own daughter, fight and win her battle against heartbreak and loneliness and, like Job, arise from her ashheap and make a new life for herself. And I have learned about love from both of them—an unqualifying love stripped of all selfish pride that is often identified with parental affection.

Sunday after Sunday, during this long and seemingly endless night, these two parents have spent their one day of rest driving almost three hundred miles just to speak their love to their exiled son; for the first six years never even sure of being allowed to see him until they got to the hospital. Such love is too much a part of the very heart of God to go unrewarded. Long ago I stopped pleading with God to restore a mental capacity lost at birth and to just give us back the lovable, childish boy we had known.

This has been done, although the night is not entirely over and the fight goes on. New drugs, new methods of therapy, and new understanding of the need for sick minds to be given the same loving care as sick bodies have unlocked his torture chamber. All this we see as answers to our prayers, just more evidence of God's unfailing love.

Although my dear ones are only a part of a vast army of such burdened parents, the path they walk is still a lonely one. Grief such as theirs must be shut away from a world of people that cannot understand until they, too, are handed Abraham's knife. For some that burden is too heavy to carry and they should not be censured when they try to find forgetfulness. Yet there lives a prayer of thanks in my heart that mine have come into a consciousness of God's eternal presence, his love and wisdom. For them forgetfulness is unnecessary in the remembrance that they do not walk alone.

13.

A Question
of Life or Death

A YOUNG FRIEND with a strong faith in God believes that life and death should be called by just the opposite names—that what we call life is actually death, and life is yet to come for us who think we are now living. Who can say if she is right or wrong?

There are individuals who claim to have knowledge of the existence that awaits us after the experience we call death, but the Bible does not support any of their theories. We only know in part and prophesy in part, Paul wrote to the Corinthians, "for now we see through a glass darkly." And in Hebrews we read a reference to this experience as entering "into that within the veil" (6:19).

By our standards, a "veil" indicates a very fine line between the living and the dead, if we accept immortality as a fact. And that tenet, of course, is the very foundation of the Christian's faith. Whether the "glass" is less dark from the other side we cannot say, but many sincere believers have had experiences that indicate it may be.

The Bible also supports this belief, in both Old and New Testaments. The death of Moses is one case in point. Historians say he was not permitted to enter the land for which he searched so long, and Moses himself, resigned to that fact, told the Israelites, "The Lord hath said unto me, Thou shalt not go over this Jordan" (Deut. 31:2). Yet if we follow Moses in his last days we find he did enter that land in spirit, if not in body.

After writing new laws for his people and then delivering his beautiful swan song, which included the reminder, "The eternal God is thy refuge, and underneath are the everlasting arms" (Deut. 33: 27), the old man went alone up Mount Nebo, as the divine voice had directed him to do. There the Lord showed him the land he had been forbidden to enter. Standing on the highest peak of the mountain, perhaps in the first golden glow of dawn, Moses looked over the land of his dreams—"all the land of Gilead, unto Dan . . . the land of Ephraim and Manasseh, and all the land of Judah. . . ."

But these divisions in Canaan had not yet been made! Moses had to be looking through the eyes of faith, knowing that the dream he had lived with for so long would be fulfilled. But who can say whether his "beholding" of the land came before or after death? Or that Moses did not enter that land in spirit, along with those who went in the flesh? If Moses wrote the Book of Deuteronomy, as is generally accepted, he wrote the account of his own death and made the statement that he was buried (apparently by the Lord) in a "valley in the land of Moab . . . but no man knoweth of his sepulchre unto this day" (Deut. 34:6). Again we wonder: Did Moses write this account of his own death from a prophetic vision, or after having experienced it? No man has the answer.

We do know, however, that this triumphant transition of Moses not only supports faith in a continuing existence but also the comforting belief that all unfulfilled dreams, any unfinished life's work, can be brought into completion after our bodies are discarded. When a torch of faith, the flame of which has been lighted by divine spirit, has to be laid down, another runner in time snatches it up and the race goes on to a triumphant conclusion. To those like Moses, truly dedicated to a dream, only the race is important, not the winner who carries the torch at the end.

At about the age of eight I shocked my mother by declaring I didn't want to go to heaven when I died. "All people do there is play harps," I defended my position, "and I can't play a harp."

Heaven had been made to sound just that boring to me—nothing to do but wander around forever and forever on streets of gold. Now I know (through the eyes of faith) that in my continuing existence I can learn to play a harp if I want to; or sing the songs I never had the voice for on earth; or write the books I take along with me in my heart.

The Bible is rich in legends and texts to give faith to the continuity of life, and the illusion of the experience we call death. It has to be an illusion if life continues.

Shortly before the end of World War II, an old lady I loved said wistfully, knowing she hadn't much longer on earth, "I'm not afraid to die, but I wish I could stay around and see all the marvelous new inventions they say are coming."

She didn't "stay around" very long after that, but now as I watch television, see a jet plane streak across the sky faster than sound, read of the wonders performed through new drugs and new surgical skills and about men walking in space and orbiting the moon, she seems very close. And I like to think that my mother, like Moses, sees all the things she longed to see in her continuing life—beauty where we on this side of the veil see only ashes, and peace for a world in turmoil that our human eyes fail to see as fact.

Six years ago the word came that my oldest brother, a devout church worker living in a Texas city, had succumbed to a heart attack. Stunned by the news, I had sat at my desk after the phone call ended, trying to think of this vital, outgoing personality as being cold and still in death. It couldn't be, I thought. The man who by his energizing faith had stayed young in heart at eighty-three could not be through living. Then suddenly I was recalling our last visit together, five years before, and feeling closer to him than during the years we had been separated only by distance.

The two of us were reminiscing, as older people often do when they get together, and the subject came up of our baby sister who had died about sixty years before. We had both been devoted to the two-year-old tot, but my brother, around fifteen at the time of her long illness, had more vivid recollections of her than I.

"Sis," he'd said that day, "I'm going to tell you something I've never told a soul, not even my wife. It always seemed too fantastic to believe, yet I swear it's God's truth. Even after all these years I can see it as clearly as I did that night."

Then he told me this story about the baby's death. Another brother, three years younger than he, was visiting on a farm about five miles from our Texas home when the baby's condition became so critical that our father sent the older boy in the family buggy to bring the younger one home. It was almost night by the time the two boys started the drive home. When darkness fell, the younger one dozed but the older one was too disturbed about the baby, who had been his special pet, to relax.

"I figure it must have been right around nine o'clock," he told me, "for we'd left the farm at eight and were within about a mile of home, when suddenly she was there, right in front of me, so real I started to call out to her. Then I realized it couldn't be my baby sister I was staring at. This baby's face wasn't pale and emaciated as hers had been after being sick so long, but round and rosy with health. Yet the eyes . . ."

He choked a little, almost overcome with emotion at the remembrance, then went on. "They were the eyes, all right. Remember what a deep blue they were? Yet they weren't a baby's eyes any more. They were old, if you know what I mean. Old and wise, as though she knew things far beyond the rest of us. As wise as time. Then she smiled and I had no more doubts. Remember the deep dimples she had? It was our little sister all right, and I half rose in the buggy seat, reaching for her, but then she vanished as suddenly as she'd appeared."

Although frightened and bewildered, he had known in his heart that the baby was dead. When he reached home and our father had come out of the house at the sound of the buggy wheels, my brother hadn't waited for him to speak but had asked, "When, Papa?" Told the child had died about a half hour before, he knew he had not dreamed the whole thing.

"It scared me," he said, "so I never could tell anyone about it. I admit it scares me even yet. What do you think I saw that night, Sis?"

"You saw her," I told him. "You were thinking of her, and when her spirit left its body, it went straight to you."

My brother, slightly more orthodox in his views than I, was silent for a long moment. Then he said thoughtfully, "I wonder."

Now, I had the comforting thought five years later, he did not have to wonder any more. He had his answers. Our little sister had not died, only discarded a body too damaged to be of further use to her.

The very morning before the night my father lay down in his yard and quietly died, he came into the kitchen, beaming happily. "Do you suppose dogs go to heaven?" he asked my mother.

She had replied a little impatiently, "Of course not. Why do you ask such a silly question?"

"Because old Trust has been following me around for days, barking at my heels," he startled us by replying. Trust was the name of a sheep dog he'd owned as a rancher in west Texas, before he became a minister. Before I was born. It had been at least fifty years since the dog had been mentioned, but as the day passed and Papa showed no further signs of mental aberration, we forgot his childish question until he was found about dusk, cold in death. Then I wondered. Had that dog been a warning sent him?

In Tulsa, over a hundred miles away, my youngest sister and her husband were preparing to entertain friends at dinner in their home. She had asked him to run a last-minute errand for her, but when she left the kitchen she found him sitting in the living room, his small dog on his lap. When she asked why he hadn't gone, my brother-in-law replied quite seriously, "Because Beans [the little dog] tells me there won't be any party here tonight. He doesn't say why, but I think he knows."

The phone rang at that moment and I was on the line, telling them about Papa. One great Mind, not many minds as we think. One great Love, encompassing all. That is the only explanation I have.

Because I had suffered from severe uremia while carrying my second child, he was born with a jaundiced condition that made me live with fear for the almost three years we were permitted to keep him—and made him precious beyond words, as every parent of a handicapped child can understand.

His final illness lasted six weeks. For ten days before he was released he had lain in a state of paralysis, unable to move or speak or swallow. Only his eyes could tell me he was mindful of my presence, but because they did, I couldn't bear to leave his side, day or night.

The night of his passing, my mother saw he was sinking and summoned the doctor without telling me. When he came, he examined the child, shook his head, and then went into the kitchen with my husband to await developments. Refusing Mamma's plea to retire and let her keep watch, I did consent to lie down across the bed where the baby lay, although not close enough to disturb him.

Too exhausted to sleep, I was still wide awake when I saw him move. My heart leaped as he turned his wasted little body completely over so that he was very near me. Then a thin little hand, icy cold, reached out and touched my face in a familiar caress. Clearly and distinctly he spoke two words: "Sweet Mommy."

My wild cry of joy brought the others quickly. "He moved and spoke!" I told them. "He must be better."

The doctor bent over him, then looked at me anxiously. "He couldn't have," he said gently. "The child is gone. Already cold."

But I knew then and know still that it happened just as I have said. Was it with his last breath that my child had spoken his love for me? Or after death claimed him? For so long I wondered, but not any more. Before or after makes no difference, for there is no death.

It was shortly before the passing of a beloved sister that I was given a vision of how beautiful the transition we call death can be. At least I think of it as a vision, although actually it came as a dream.

She had suffered for years with a lingering malignancy, and for the last year of her life I had shared that suffering with her, helping a devoted, unselfish sister-in-law care for her. It had been a trying experience to watch her body wasting away, so slowly and so painfully; yet it had also been a rewarding experience to see her unwavering faith in God and her dauntless courage.

My dream had to be symbolic, I felt. In it I saw an ugly, misshapen vase standing on a table, plainly an example of primitive earthen pottery such as ancient Indian craftsmen might have made. Drab, without any semblance of beauty.

As I looked at it, wondering why it had been preserved, a great hand, unattached to a body, reached out and touched the ugly vessel, lovingly, gently. Then before my very eyes it was suddenly transformed into a thing of beauty, both in color and design—a rare, lovely work of art, from which a glow emanated that gave it the look of having been made of gold.

The picture of that transformation still lives vividly in memory, an assurance that there is no end to life, only a new beginning.

Wherever and whatever heaven is—an actual place or a state of consciousness—the passing of a friend a few years ago demonstrated there is nothing to fear on the other side of the veil. This friend was hospitalized with pneumonia, which we did not consider serious until I called her room one day and was told by her nurse that she had just died and was then being taken from the room.

After spreading the word among our mutual friends, several of us went to offer condolences to her mother, only to learn to our delight that it had been a mistake. Nellie was still alive. As her body was being taken to the service elevator after her presumed death, a doctor had stopped the orderlies and had her taken into an operating room where he opened her chest and massaged her heart until it started beating again.

Three days later we again received word that Nellie was dead. It was at her funeral that her pastor told this story: He had gone to see her after life had been restored following her first "death." She had greeted him with a glowing face as she cried happily, "O pastor, this is such a beautiful place! More beautiful than I ever dreamed it could be."

Where was she when she said those words? Surely not lying on a hospital bed in a sanitarily colorless room. Though men of science had temporarily restored life to her body, she no longer had need of that body. She had been set free. Perhaps, having glimpsed the beauty of the "land beyond" she had not wanted to come back. I like to think that was it.

Surely there is no greater evidence needed that ours is a living God than the timelessness of time, the eternality of the life cycle and the love force influencing human hearts. And no greater proof is needed of the unreality of death than the words of Jesus where he said, "If a man keep my saying [teaching] he shall never see death" (John 8:51).

The sum of all his teachings was for men to know, honor, and love God, the Giver of life. Then, indeed, death becomes only a shadow that we need not fear. Just another experience of living.

14.

The Light
That Goes Before Us

WHILE RIDING with my nephew on a two-lane high-way not long ago, we saw a pickup truck overloaded with heavy scrap lumber coming towards us. As the other vehicle drew closer we saw a big piece of timber on the top of the load start sliding off, unknown to the driver. It was falling toward us, and I saw with dreadful certainty as we drew opposite the other vehicle that the long 4 x 4 would strike us just at an angle to smash, if not penetrate, the windshield.

My driver saw it, too. Floorboarding the gas pedal, he shot us past the truck right under that falling timber. We heard it hit the pavement directly behind us.

For a moment as he slowed the car to a legal speed, neither of us spoke. Then he drew a long breath and said, "Well, it looks like somebody upstairs is on the job."

This incident is typical of my life. "Somebody upstairs," as that youth expressed it, has been guarding me for three-quarters of a century, averting death and disaster time and time again by just that narrow a margin. And saving me over and over from the results of my human errors. Is it any wonder my heart longs to praise God? It's been a long, and at times a rough, road, but the prophet Isaiah sums up my life story (which this book is not meant to be) where he says, "They that wait upon [depend upon] the Lord shall renew their strength; they shall mount up with wings as eagles; they shall run and not be weary; and they shall walk and not faint" (Isa. 40:31).

There have been many times when I walked so free my feet did not

117

seem to touch the ground, times I could run my race without consciousness of fatigue or discouragement, and many times that I walked slowly—so slow and painfully I seemed to make no progress. But looking back over my shoulder at the irregular path I've traveled, I can see I never was alone, for shadowy forms of those who walked that same path ahead of me are reflected in the luminous glow of the incandescent lamp of truth that has given light for my feet.

The living Christ has walked with me also, often without my conscious awareness, not only beside me for companionship but before me for guidance and behind me for protection.

In the early fall of 1960, that guiding light was going before me the day that I was literally stopped from buying a new wool suit. I was walking out of my door to attend a sale at a reliable store when a voice deep inside me said, "No." It was too clear and plain to ignore, so I went back inside and sat down with my Bible, asking for light. I needed the suit for winter wear, and the one advertised seemed just right in price and in style. Surely I was wrong in thinking I was being directed to pass up this opportunity. Hadn't I long since accepted as fact that God wanted my happiness in all things?

Yet as my short prayer ended and I opened the Bible at random, I found to my surprise that I was reading in Ezekiel, a book I seldom consciously selected. And the message I was reading was very disturbing: "Therefore, thou son of man, prepare thee stuff for removing . . . for thou shalt remove from thy place to another place" (12:2,3).

This couldn't be a message for me, I felt. The last thing I wanted to do was move. And certainly a new suit would not add to "stuff" that might prove burdensome. Yet suddenly my anticipation in shopping was spoiled, and I decided to wait until I felt sure. It might be that God had another plan for me for that day.

A week passed, and I was feeling impatient with myself for having passed up the sale when the letter came from my daughter in Phoenix, Arizona. It told me of plans she and her husband were making to build a small apartment complex on city lots they had purchased and that their plans included me. Several years before she had asked for and received my promise that if this project ever came to pass I would move to Arizona and become their first tenant.

Now she was taking for granted that I would keep that vague promise I'd all but forgotten, and I was almost panic-stricken at the thought. I didn't want to move anywhere and certainly not to Arizona, where I'd have to build a whole new life for myself. That wouldn't be easy at the age of seventy. I had deep, deep roots in Oklahoma and a host of friends. With continued good health, such as I'd enjoyed for years, I could keep my coveted independence for many years yet.

Still, was it fair to Penny to wait until I was ready to retire? Deep in my heart I knew she'd been thinking more about me than herself in planning this venture and that she and her brothers had been worrying about my living so far from all of them in my advancing years. This seemed to her an ideal solution. I'd live very close to her but still have my own home. Of course it would be wonderful to live so near my only daughter, but I did not want my life or my work disrupted just yet. I'd go in a few years, but not yet.

It was when I sat down to write her my decision that I recalled the suit I'd almost bought, but hadn't. In the warm desert winters a wool suit such as I'd had in mind would be rarely worn, but if I moved, the hundred and fifty dollars I'd almost spent would be needed. Was that why I'd been stopped? Not just because of the useless expenditure, but to remind me in this hour of what God's will for me was?

O please, please, not yet, I found myself praying, and like an answer came the echo of the words in Ezekiel, *"Prepare thee stuff for removing."* There was no longer any doubt. This was something God wanted me to do, and I must trust him to know what was right. So I wrote Penny that I would be ready to move Christmas week, since she had suggested she and her husband could come after me with a U-Haul trailer during the holidays and I could stay with them if the apartments were not quite ready.

As I began to prepare my "stuff" for moving, however, it was in a spirit of resignation instead of anticipation. Although my heart told me this was God's will for me, it was a continual battle to relinquish my own will. Pulling up roots became increasingly painful as friends began pressuring me not to go—not using words only, but acts of love that often made me sit down in the middle of packing boxes and shed bitter tears. Though I went to the telephone more than once to call Penny and say I'd changed my mind, yet never was I quite able to put the call through. Over and over I prayed to be shown the light, and always my answer was remembrance of that verse of Scripture read out of context, followed by the conviction that the light had been give me before I'd heard from Penny and that I must trust in it.

Another call came from Penny a few days before Christmas. She told me they had sold their home and were moving into a small one-bedroom place until the apartments were finished, but they would come and get me anyway and I could sleep on the living room divan for a month or so. Now I was panic-stricken again at the thought that I must have mistaken my guidance. Maybe I should have trusted my own desires! It was too late for that, however, because my apartment was rented and the new tenants eager to move in; I'd sold some of my heavier pieces of furniture and everything else was packed; I'd had a round of farewell parties given me and gifts showered upon me. How could I find another apartment and stay in Oklahoma City after all that? Besides, my son and his wife were coming for Christmas to see Penny and her husband and help load the U-Haul. I had to go now!

Yet what would I do about my work for the next few weeks, maybe months? It had been wholly neglected during my weeks of preparations for moving and my disturbed mental state. There would be no chance to set up my typewriter and files at the crowded little house three people would be living in. If it was spring before the new buildings were finished, as Penny had hinted it might be, not only would I be out of money but might have lost some good markets. Surely, surely, I had made a terrible mistake in interpreting that message as applying to myself!

Not knowing whether to be glad or sorry that it looked as though I'd been stopped from moving, only too aware of the impossibility of renting anything in Phoenix at the height of the winter tourist season, I told Penny I would decide what to do and let her know. Leaving the telephone, I sat down on a crate and was staring at the confusion around me, thinking of the neglected assignments in the box on which I sat, when I heard the mailman in the hall. A few minutes later I was reading an airmail letter from a friend who had been a former member of my prayer group. She had moved to Arizona several years before and now lived near a small town about seventy miles from Phoenix. As I read my last doubts vanished. Here was all the proof I needed that God wanted me to move. My friend, knowing nothing of my circumstances except that I planned to move to Phoenix when the apartments were finished, was writing to tell me about a small furnished house not far from her own. A friend of hers had recently purchased the house, and it could be rented if by any chance I wanted to move before Penny was ready for me—and if I wouldn't mind living in the desert.

God going before us to prepare the way! How could I doubt any longer? What did it matter that I'd be living alone in that strange country and without transportation? Seeing God's handiwork in the timing of this offer, I didn't even wonder what the house would be like as I hurriedly wrote my letter of acceptance and went out to mail it. That night I called Penny to tell her my plans. She agreed it was the perfect arrangement. They could drop me off there, with whatever I'd need, then store the rest of my things in Phoenix. She then broke the news to me that she hadn't had the heart to tell me sooner. Work had been stopped on their project until they found additional financing. "But don't worry," she'd added in typical Penny style; "God will show us the way and everything will work out all right."

How Penny's faith was rewarded is her own story. Suffice it to say that when she got back to Phoenix, after leaving me in my new desert home, she found her problem had been resolved, and in a most unusual way. Hearing her news, I thought of God's covenant with Abraham when he said, "Get thee out of thy country [out of Haran] . . . unto a land that I will show thee . . . and I will bless thee . . . and . . . bless them that bless thee" (Gen. 12:1–3).

Because God's leading is always perfect, my three-months desert sojourn proved to be one of the happiest and most productive periods of my life. The small house I'd rented in faith was comfortable in every way, with a big picture window that made an ideal place for my typewriter, though I have to admit that work was sometimes forgotten as I sat there entranced with the panorama of life outside: Tiny ground squirrels at play, acting like frolicsome little boys; a woodpecker seeking water from a giant Saguaro cactus standing like a gnarled sentry beside my little house; roadrunners coming fearlessly for the crumbs I put out; a family of quail trailing across the yard in single file; a blue-jay scolding from a Palo Verde tree.

Life, always life. The desert, with no other house in sight, was teeming with it. So how could I feel alone even when I didn't see a human being for days at a time? Even at night there was the sound of life in the yapping of coyotes, some of which came close enough to the house that on moonlight nights I could see their shadowy forms. Just the same, I felt safe and secure in the refuge God had sent me to.

God seemed very near, very real, during those days. He was in the breathtakingly beautiful sunsets, for only his hand could paint such vivid colors and designs along the horizon. He was in the fantastic vegetation, walking with me for hours among cacti so grotesque they assumed a beauty peculiarly their own. He spoke to me in the brooding stillness and always of his love for all life. When I left to go to my new home in Phoenix, it was with mingled regret and anticipation but with deep gratitude for the restful and productive interim God had given me.

It was almost three years later before I was given the real reason why God had ordained that I should move to Arizona to be near my daughter. It was she who was with me when I suffered what at first was diagnosed as a major heart attack, she who rushed me to the hospital and spent anxious hours by my bedside during the week I lay under oxygen and the two weeks of clinical tests that followed. It was her faith that strengthened mine when the specialist she had called in gave his diagnosis. My heart condition resulted from a severe hiatal hernia which had allowed the stomach to invade the chest area, crowding against the heart. That meant complete invalidism—bed rest, a rigid diet, and medication for the rest of my life.

"If you were twenty years younger we would operate," the physician explained. "But such surgery is much too involved, too dangerous, for a person your age. You wouldn't have a fifty-fifty chance."

Stunned, I listened to words I couldn't accept. "Will I be able to work? To type?" I asked, groping for a straw to hold to.

"Certainly not." He was very emphatic. "Your working days are over. You're lucky to be alive."

"And you want me just to stay in bed and do nothing?" I remonstrated, as though he were arbitrarily passing sentence upon me. "I don't call that living."

"Maybe not," he said stiffly, "but you have no choice. It's all we can offer you."

Long after quietness settled over the hospital that night, I lay sleepless, listening to the echo of those words, pulsing through me like my erratic heartbeats: *You have no choice . . . no choice.* But a man had said that, not God. Didn't He always give us a choice? For so long his love had protected me. Wasn't he still just as ready as always to save me from becoming a useless burden to my loved ones?

I do have a choice, I finally thought, a vast relief making my tense body relax. I can choose to die if I can't honor God by living. I won't do that to Penny! I can't, God. I can't.

It was then a vaguely remembered verse of Scripture touched my mind, as gently as though it had wings. "The Lord said that he would dwell in the thick darkness" (1 Kings 8:12). Words spoken by Solomon reminded me that I was not alone, that the same Lord God shared my darkness with me.

Then other winged words flashed through my mind like pinpoints of brilliant light—bits from the Psalms I love: "In the night his song shall be with me. . . . Sing unto him a new song. . . ."

A new song, a new life. Did it matter where that life would be spent or how? It would be good, for God would continue to direct it, to keep a song in my heart.

The thought filled me with such elation, such a sense of triumph, that I felt my spirit must already have left my damaged body and be floating upon soft cumulus clouds, completely immersed in divine love. It was as though I had gone back in time and again stood in a swift river, feeling the caress of soft water over my face. Or was it soft hands? Again I heard my father's deep voice saying gently, "Just hold to my hand and trust God."

The next morning I told my physician I wanted the operation, regardless of the risks. He protested and called in Penny, who said only, "It's my mother's life and her choice." But something in her face and voice made me know she had shared my hours of "thick darkness" and found God there, just as I had.

Exactly one week after the complicated surgery, which also included the removal of a highly inflamed gall bladder which was on the point of rupture from one huge stone, I went to my own home, sitting beside my son-in-law in his car.

God continued to be very near, very real, during my convalescence. We talked together or sang together during the night when pain or irregular heartbeat made sleep elusive. He walked with me when I began the daily exercises prescribed by my physician; he planted new creative ideas and dreams in my mind and heart to fill up the empty days.

Truly David sang of an eternal God, just as cognizant of a troubled world today as of the troubled world in which the psalmist lived when he wrote,

> Sing to God, sing praises to his name;
>   lift up a song to him who rides upon the clouds;
> . . . .
> Father of the fatherless and protector of widows
>   is God in his holy habitation.
> God gives the desolate a home to dwell in;
>   he leads out the prisoners to prosperity;
>   but the rebellious dwell in a parched land.
>
> (Psalm 68:4-6, RSV)

Ours, then, is the choice of the type of "land," or life, we dwell in, for when we open our hearts for him to enter in and live with us, there can be no need, spiritual or material, that he will not help us meet.

15.
Living in Christ

ON A NIGHT in April 1968, when the city of Washington, D.C., was paralyzed by one of the most destructive race riots our nation had yet known, I sat in the banquet room of a hotel only about six blocks from the area being devastated by fire and looting, together with almost two hundred delegates to a national convention. A 4:00 P.M. curfew and blocked streets not only kept us there as virtual prisoners but also kept away the majority of delegates that had been expected, including speakers who were to present the evening programs.

That night we were making a valiant effort to carry on, since there was nothing else we could do; yet it was far from being the happy occasion we had anticipated. In spite of gay table decorations and formal dinner gowns, tension produced a pall as tangible as the cloud of smoke hanging over the city, evidenced in forced smiles, nervous chatter, and fear-filled eyes.

Although the hastily drafted substitute speaker was extremely interesting, it was hard to give her our undivided attention with police sirens and wails of ambulances reminding us of the chaos in the streets. Hard, too, to forget the horror with which we had watched televised scenes during the day—street battles, terrified people fleeing from burning buildings, the looting and sniping and overturning of cars—that depicted the violence aroused by the assassination of Dr. Martin Luther King.

It was still early when the speaker sat down. Reluctant to return to our rooms and those shocking TV pictures, we all welcomed the suggestion of an impromptu songfest. A volunteer pianist and a song leader mounted the platform, and several familiar songs were sung half-heartedly.

Then suddenly the atmosphere changed as the pianist struck the opening bars of "How Great Thou Art." It was as though she had struck a chord upon every heart present. With one accord we began singing praises to the God we had temporarily forgotten in our anxiety. By the time the song ended, faces were relaxed, eyes glowing, fears forgotten.

That hour marked the beginning of an assembly that will long live in the memory of those who were there. With fear routed and faith revived, the next four days were marked by a spiritual fellowship such as none of us had ever felt before at a prearranged secular convention.*

This is the power in praise. It is a reminder that God reigns over a world we are prone to forget is his creation, that cannot therefore be destroyed as long as he is recognized as "our strength and our salvation." And it is a reminder that the God we worship has greater power than that generated through the submerged violence of men unattuned to love.

Recalling that unforgettable night brings me the remembrance of the prayer of praise King David made before his troubled people: "Thine, O Lord, is the greatness and the power and the glory, and the victory." Victory over internal strife in our great country can be ours if every disturbed heart will echo David's prayer of praise, bringing peace to his own mind. Peace cannot be a reality unless it has its roots in hearts, not in minds that are intent upon "pointing the finger" at unhappy conditions or circumstances rather than pointing toward the power released in trusting a God of love.

The greatest need in our confused social structure today is to have hearts filled with praise, lending power to our prayers, creating an atmosphere of positive faith that God lives and knows the needs of every human soul—to worship him as a living presence rather than a dry theological fact.

---

*Reprinted by permission from *Sunday Digest:* © 1970, David C. Cook Publishing Co., Elgin, Ill., from devotional article by author.

Now as I write the conclusion to a sketchy, but honest, account of reasons why there is a continual song of praise in my own heart, even at times when my path is not as smooth as I would like it to be, I am sitting on my patio just as the sun comes up to flood a shadowy world with light. It is a familiar phenomenon of nature, yet one that never ceases to be awe-inspiring for me. Light emerging from darkness, day replacing night, faculties revived after the resting period of sleep—the story of life retold.

This sunrise seems to speak a special message to me, for it speaks of another beginning, after a prolonged inactivity forced upon me as the result of overtaxing the damaged heart I have lived with for eight years. Eight productive years, in spite of times of discouragement, when I have found self-fulfillment in offering praise for the loving presence that renews my strength when I become weak. Years in which I have learned more fully than ever to say with Paul "It is no longer I who live, but Christ who lives in me; and the life I now live in the flesh I live by faith" (Gal. 2:20, RSV).

Not that I have to any degree reached the state of perfection that Jesus taught is possible and that Paul says we should "reach toward," only that I am constantly made aware that there is growth and development in the reaching process. What is growth except trial and error and the challenge of faith?

So what if a physical weakness slows me down at times? What if advancing age causes others to see limitations that my spirit refuses to recognize? What if the road my feet have been forced to walk upon seems unbearably lonely at times? Loneliness has no real power where there is knowledge that we are never alone, that an indwelling Christ is always close, ready to lend us his strength when ours fails.

In Ecclesiastes 3, the preacher (presumed to be Solomon) reminds us that there is system and order in a God-created world: "To everything there is a season, . . . a time to plant, and a time to pluck up that which is planted . . . a time to keep silence and a time to speak . . . ." Since God has again spared me to continue praising him, I know this is still the season of planting for me, not a time for silence. It is a time for singing, not for mourning over past mistakes or for entertaining fears for the future. It is a time of spring, no matter what the calendar says. Spring is not a date, after all. It is a mood of nature, or of mind—the Resurrection relived.

As though to offer me another reminder that God means for all his created to know peace and joy, a mocking bird trills a joyous greeting to the rising sun from an orange tree. "It's a good world," he seems to be singing. "Men should not be afraid to live joyously and fully, as God destined they should. Hearts should sing the praises of God and live in peace."

This whimsical thought again opens the treasure chest I label memory, and I find myself smiling as I look at an almost forgotten mental picture of a young girl giving her high school graduation address. She stands before the podium of the small church that is the largest in her small town, but not on tiptoe in eager anticipation of entering a new world as such graduates are supposed to do. Instead, her feet are planted firmly, her girlish face is intent and serious. Having recently joined the church as insurance against eternal punishment of some vaguely unreal thing called her soul, she has chosen as her theme a solemn renunciation of the world.

Since this renunciation included her secret dream of becoming a writer instead of a school teacher, as fate seemed to decree for her, she makes, perhaps unconsciously, the address her swan song by writing it in the form of poetry. At least she and her impressed audience regarded it as poetry, although in time she came to realize that in the literary scene it would more accurately have been labeled doggerel.

Perhaps it is not strange that after these more than sixty years I can recall only the opening two lines of this first literary effort: "Life is a school with its students of men, And the Almighty Father to teach us." Nor did I realize, as I wrote the jingling lines, how prophetically I was speaking.

As dreary as I envisioned a Christian's life to be, based on the impressions of my early youth, I did not understand that the lessons I would find so hard to learn would not be assigned by the Great Teacher, but by myself. Nor that they would be lessons of love, hard only because it would take me so long to let him liberate me from self-pity and frustration and self-imposed limitations, so long to accept God's merciful love that eventually gave me back the dream I had rejected as being opposed to a Christian way of life.

All dreams, I had to learn, are of God if they are born of the soul's sincere desire; all can be realized to whatever extent faith in ourselves as God's instruments of expression dictates.

But even God-given dreams can be self-destructive where there is a lack of faith, and if we feel only self-concern and self-responsibility in making the dream come true. Only when we let God reign over our lives can any of us know peace and an indestructible security. Only when we go within and contact the ever present God-Power can we find true self-fulfillment.

It is awareness of need within our human selves that makes us reach for God's always available helping Hand. This is why the poor and the needy can be not the underprivileged, but the privileged. There is no fulfillment in life comparable to the security and contentment that comes from putting complete trust in God.

Another writer has expressed so well and with such clarity and poignancy the thoughts I have tried to bring that I am borrowing her lines to use as my epilogue:

NO OTHER WAY

Could we but see the pattern of our days,
We should discern how devious were the ways
By which we came to this, the present time,
This place in life; and we should see the climb
Our soul has made up through the years.
We should forget the hurts, the wanderings, the fears,
The wastelands of our life and know
That we could come no other way or grow
Into our good without these steps our feet
Found hard to take, our faith found hard to meet.
The road of life winds on, and we like travelers go
From turn to turn until we come to know
The truth that life is endless and that we
Forever are inhabitants of all eternity.

MARTHA SMOCK

(Used by permission of *Daily Word,* United School of Christianity)